Sport Management Library

SPORT MANAGEMENT FIELD EXPERIENCES

Jacquelyn Cuneen & M. Joy Sidwell
Bowling Green State University

FITNESS INFORMATION TECHNOLOGY, INC.
P.O. BOX 4425, UNIVERSITY AVE.
MORGANTOWN, WV 26504

Library of Congress Catalog Card Number: 94-72328

ISBN 1-885693-01-X

Cover Design: James M. Williams
Copyeditor: Sandra R. Woods
Printed by: BookCrafters

Printed in the United States of America
10 9 8 7 6 5 4 3 2

Fitness Information Technology, Inc.
P. O. Box 4425, University Avenue
Morgantown, WV 26504 USA
(800)-477-4348
(304)-599-3482

SPORT MANAGEMENT LIBRARY

The **SPORT MANAGEMENT LIBRARY** is an integrative textbook series, targeted toward undergraduate students. The textbooks included in the library are reflective of the content areas prescribed by the NASPE/NASSM curriculum standards for undergraduate programs in sport management.

FORTHCOMING TITLES IN THE SPORT MANAGEMENT LIBRARY

Case Studies in Sport Marketing
Communication in Sport Organizations
Ethics in Sport Management
Financing Sport
Fundamentals of Legal and Risk Management in Sport
Fundamentals of Sport Marketing
Management Essentials in Sport Organizations
Sport Facility Planning and Management
Sport Governance in the Global Community

Jacquelyn Cuneen, Ed. D., is Sport Management Field Experience Coordinator at Bowling Green State University. Her primary research foci are professional preparation in sport management and sport and event marketing. She has authored or co-authored articles appearing in the *Journal of Sport Management, Sex Roles, Sport Marketing Quarterly, Journal of Physical Education, Recreation, and Dance, Schole*, and others. Prior to coming to BGSU, she was Account Executive, Continuity Director and Director of Women's Programming for two ABC Radio affiliates in New York's Capitol District, and Southern Tier. She has been a member of the NASSM Executive Council, the Graduate Sport Management Program Advisory Board for West Virginia University, and various other professional committees. Dr. Cuneen was a visiting scholar for the North Carolina Center for Independent Higher Education in 1992.

M. Joy Sidwell, M. A., is Chair of Bowling Green State University's internationally renown Sport Management program. Her primary research and teaching foci have been sport history and professional preparation in sport management. Her research has been published in the *Journal of Sport Management, Sex Roles*, and *Journal of Physical Education, Recreation, and Dance*, among others. She has also authored or co-authored textbook chapters addressing sport history and professional preparation. She was BGSU's first Field Experience Coordinator, and built the field experience component into one of the country's most recognized and respected sport management experiential education programs. Ms. Sidwell has served in an advisory capacity to several new sport management programs in the United States.

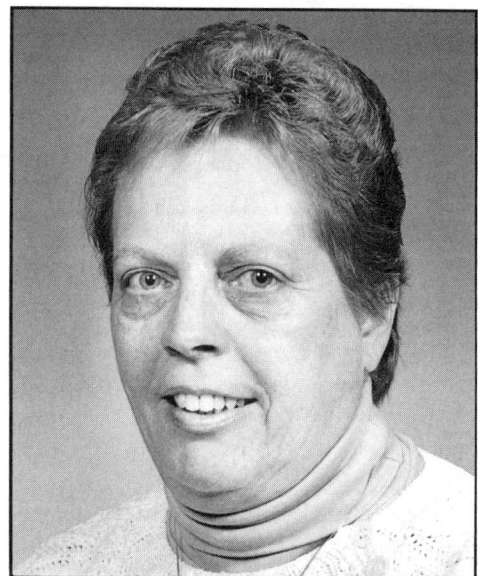

SPORT MANAGEMENT FIELD EXPERIENCES

Table of Contents

Preface

Sport Management Field Experiences addresses the experiential component contained in the National Association for Sport and Physical Education/North American Society for Sport Management (NASPE/NASSM) sport management program standards. Although *Sport Management Field Experiences* is a compilation of information based on field experience procedures used by several institutions, the main concepts are based primarily on the field experience curriculum used by Bowling Green State University (Ohio). BGSU conducts a large sport management program consisting of approximately 450 undergraduate and 20 graduate students per year. BGSU faculty have been supervising approximately 130 field experience students per year since the early 1980s. The field experience component of the BGSU sport management program has been modified numerous times to reflect the most currently useful aspects of experiential education. The field experience curriculum has been used as a model by several new North American sport management programs and by established programs revising their experiential components.

Sport Management Field Experiences attempts to answer those questions most frequently asked by sport management students, their families, friends, and support groups. The book is intended to be an introduction to the purposes of field experiences, site search methods, credentials preparation, interview processes, conduct of field experiences, and appropriate academic exercises. The book is not intended to be the sole source addressing the body of practical field experience knowledge. Students will need faculty advising, career counseling, and other professional interactions in order to search, screen, accept, and successfully complete sport management field experiences. Throughout the book, students are encouraged to seek assistance from numerous sources, but the prevalent message is that the main responsibility in experiential readiness and learning rests with students themselves.

Students are encouraged to be pro-active in their planning, searching, and completing of field experiences. Students ask frequently about the meaning of field experiences, and Part I introduces students to experiential education and typical patterns of sport management field education. To provide students with help in choosing sites, Part II focuses on common characteristics of field experiences and guides students through the most viable ways to prepare for, search for, and receive quality field experiences. Other common questions posed by students regard résumé preparation and application strategies; Part III offers students advice on preparing their sport management credentials and addresses typical interviewing processes. Parts I, II, and III contain suggested activities for students to use in preparing themselves for their field experience term(s). Students must be aware of the reasonable expectations they should have of their supervisors. Part IV gives students the academic objectives of field experiences and lists some common ways in which they might be supported by their faculty, their site supervisors, and the organizations that sponsor their field experiences. To help students learn and observe while completing their field education, Part V provides students with several academic exercises to link classroom and practical knowledge. Appendices A through G contain examples of documents used in the conduct of sport management field experiences. Students often wish to speak with former field students and supervisors, and Appendices H1-6 provide students with chronicles from a faculty supervisor, three site supervisors, and two former field experience students.

We hope that this book makes the pursuit and completion of field experiences more amiable for both sport management students and our faculty colleagues. The book is targeted both for sport management students who are planning for their field experiences and for those already completing field experiences. The book will be most helpful to new sport management students if they acquire it early in their academic careers and refer to it often in their field experience planning and credentials preparation. Newer sport management students will gain most from the book after they have completed their introductory sport management class or during the term(s) they are enrolled in sport management pre-field experience seminars.

Portions of the book are targeted for students who are completing their field experiences and for sport management faculty who may wish to assign academic exercises to their field students. The Part V exercises have been found to be most helpful in orienting students to their field sites, and the exercises have helped students remain accountable to the academic components of their field experiences.

We gratefully acknowledge the ideas and support of the BGSU field experience supervisors: Robert E. Ammon, Jr., Cathryn L. Claussen, Sue A. Hager, Crayton L. Moss, Jerome Quarterman, and Beverly R. K. Zanger. We are equally grateful to manuscript reviewers Bonnie L. Parkhouse of Temple University and M. Elizabeth Verner of Illinois State University. Their suggestions relative to organization and comments on proposed content were especially valuable; we appreciate the attention they devoted to our project. Special thanks are extended to the Editorial Board of the Sport Management Library: Janet B. Parks, Editor-in-Chief, Gordon A. Olafson, Brenda G. Pitts, and David K. Stotlar. Their attention to guidelines and details throughout the writing stages provided us with great direction. We are especially appreciative of Fitness Information Technology, Inc. and its President, Andrew C. Ostrow, Ph.D., for the opportunity he provided to us to be part of the comprehensive series of texts addressing the content areas of the NASPE/NASSM *Sport Management Program Standards and Review Protocol* (1993).

Foreword

The sport management field experience is a valuable culminating experience for the student; it is the student's opportunity to apply the ideas and theories presented in the classroom to the experience in a work environment. Jacquelyn Cuneen and Joy Sidwell have developed a well organized and thorough text about the sport management field experience. The authors have done an exceptional job of combining their expertise and information from the Bowling Green State University field experience program with a comprehensive review of the literature relative to the field experience. The text is appropriately geared for both the sport management student (undergraduate and graduate) and the university internship coordinator.

The authors provide the student with insights into the field experience. These include planning for the field experience (i.e. investigation of sites), preparation and presentation of credentials (i.e. resumes, cover letters), and completing the field experience (i.e. responsibilities, logs, reports, culminating evaluation of the experience). The field experience text includes descriptions and discussions of many typical situations and issues which students may potentially face during field experiences. This knowledge will help students in handling the experiences with confidence and also enable students to more clearly evaluate their readiness for the experience. This text might be used as required reading for the student prior to beginning the process of searching for a field experience site.

The information contained within the text could be used by field experience coordinators when counseling, directing, and evaluating students. The appendices and figures included with the text effectively supplement the narrative portion of the text by providing valuable examples.

From the perspective of a field experience coordinator, one very helpful feature of the text is the suggested readings and activities at the end of each part. The suggested readings and activities could be used as student assignments, as part of a seminar class or as a requirement prior to their experiences in order to prepare them. Part IV offers a number of exercises relative to the managerial functions and other basic management concepts such as communication, power, influence, and change that a coordinator could incorporate into the course requirements for field experience credit.

This text is a valuable resource for sport management students and faculty, and the authors should be commended on their efforts. The text definitely contributes to the body of knowledge in sport management internships.

Darlene S. Young, Ed.D.
Associate Professor
Coordinator, Sport
Management Internships
Western Illinois University

PART I

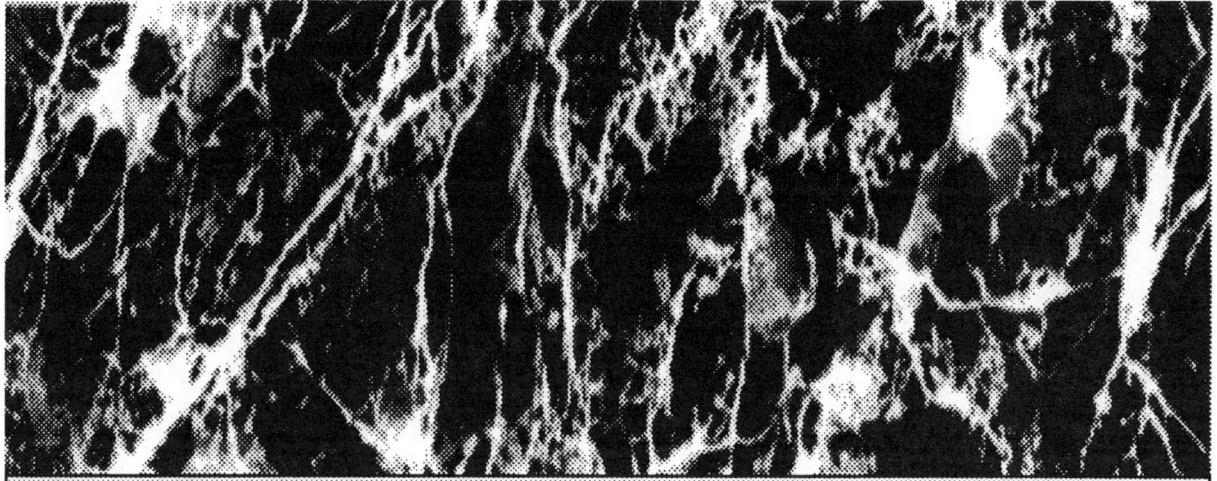

PURPOSES AND CHARACTERISTICS OF SPORT MANAGEMENT FIELD EXPERIENCES

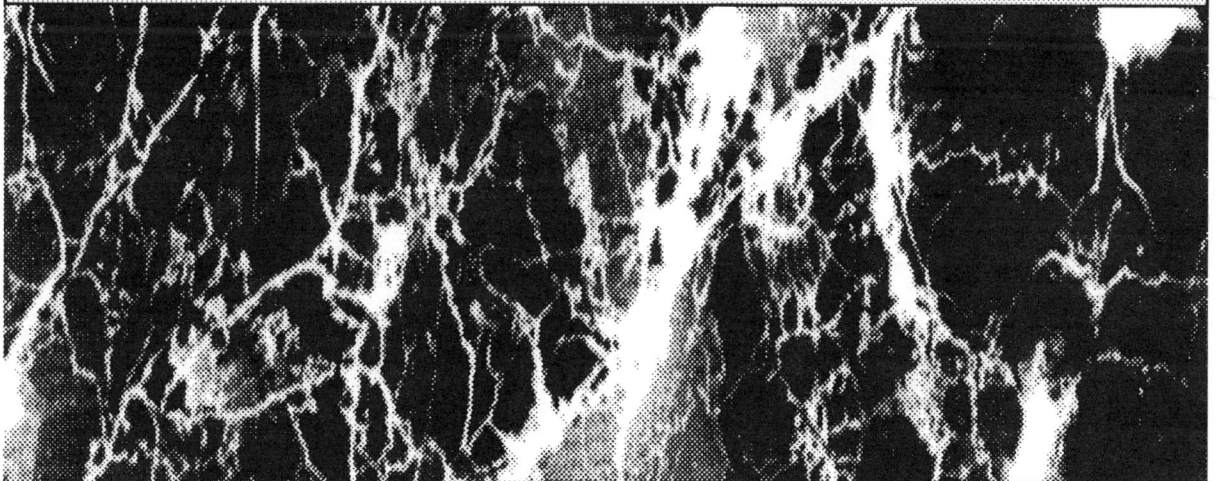

PURPOSES AND CHARACTERISTICS OF SPORT MANAGEMENT FIELD EXPERIENCES

Field experiences are essential components of the foundational professional qualifications of sport management students (Cuneen, 1992; DeSensi, Kelley, Blanton & Beitel, 1990; National Association for Sport and Physical Education/North American Society for Sport Management, 1993; Parkhouse, 1984; 1987; Parks & Quain, 1986; Parks & Zanger, 1990; Quain & Parks, 1986; Sidwell, 1984). Through field experiences, students make the transition from student to professional and are provided a link from sport management theory to practice (Sutton, 1989). Significant field experiences are vehicles by which students gain valuable, practical work experiences under the supervision of both university faculty and on-site sport management practitioners. Field experiences increase opportunities for students whose learning styles may be suited better to practical rather than classroom settings and enhance opportunities for them to become familiar with equipment and materials that could not be purchased by the institution (Verner, 1993). Field experiences enable students to add dimensions to their professional credentials, discover career options while viewing professionals in practice, and have opportunities to evaluate themselves while being evaluated by others. Field experiences provide students the means to acquire deeper commitments to their chosen fields of study, and confirm their career choices (Cuneen & Sidwell, 1993b; Sidwell, 1984). In some instances, field experiences are precursors for employment, giving students chances to demonstrate technical proficiency and providing cost-effective personnel training for industry (Ciofalo, 1992).

Washburn (1984) asserted that field experiences benefit three constituencies: students, agencies, and sponsoring institutions. Field experience students learn the necessities of taking orders, receiving directions and undertaking responsibility, and sense fulfillment in responsibility and productivity. Agencies gain from field students' time and energy, have the opportunity to observe a potential employee in meaningful situations, and gain from the students' contributions. Sponsoring institutions benefit through having doors opened for future field students, possible support (monetary or recruitment), and enhanced prestige and reputation for programs based on the demonstrated proficiency of its field students.

Experiential Education

Experiential education strategies such as sport management field experiences have existed for several decades and have been labeled using various terms, such as internships, practica, externships, clerkships, apprenticeships, and other terms as defined by specific fields of study. Generally, field experiences constitute courses that give students opportunities to be involved in work-related experiences in their major fields of study or minor/cognate areas. Although practical, field experiences are classroom extensions enabling students to gain knowledge relevant to specific fields, organizational roles, and functions.

Students, academicians, and practitioners in various areas of study view field experiences as important preludes to employment (Blensley, 1982; McClam & Kessler, 1982; Ricchiute, 1980; Taylor & Dunham, 1980). Students who have completed internships have distinct advantages in the labor market: They receive more positive evaluations and greater salaries, express greater extrinsic rewards, and have greater access to informal sources in job searches (Taylor, 1984, 1988).

Chickering (1976) described experiential education as the learning that occurs when students live through events that change their judgment, feelings, knowledge, or skills. Students need assistance when making transitions from academic to corporate sectors, and field experiences ease the jump between school and office (Bialac & Wallington, 1985). Specifically, professors are likely to teach general or theoretical approaches in preparing students for any number of corporate cultures. Emphasis on theory quite often means that academics deal with process, yet in the corporate sector, process is only as important as its output. Professional practice skills are often based more on the capacity to reflect before action than on factual knowledge or decision-making models (Schon, 1983, 1987). Problems of practitioners are complex and can not be solved simply by drawing on scientific or technical knowledge. Field experiences socialize students toward the values, norms, and cultural systems they may encounter in corporate work (Gabris & Mitchel, 1992). Parkhouse (1984) saw field experiences as opportunities for students to demonstrate competence by applying theory learned through coursework. Professional maturation and development of leadership, managerial, and self-evaluation skills are critical goals of field experiences (Sidwell, 1984). Therefore, field experience students should expect supervision and evaluation of their performances by both the college/university faculty and an on-site supervisor representing the sponsoring organization (Sidwell, 1984).

Sport Management Field Experiences

Sport management as an academic area of study began in 1966 when James G. Mason founded the first sport management major program at Ohio University (Mason, Higgins, & Wilkinson, 1981; Parks & Olafson, 1987). As the program grew, it was apparent that students needed opportunities to link theories to practice and apply classroom knowledge through faculty-supervised, pre-entry level experiences. Mason spent a sabbatical year visiting various sport corporations and convincing them of the mutual benefits of experiential education for both academe and sport enterprise. Often, students demonstrated such competency that they were hired as full-time, regular employees at the end of their experiences. Mason also found that the set of circumstances for each field experience was different. In larger sport organizations, students performed just one function (such as assistant to the ticket manager) whereas sport organizations with small administrative staffs used students in a variety of duties, such as advertising, tickets, concessions, supplies, and writing (J. G. Mason, personal communication, April 29, 1993).

Currently, there are approximately 180 institutions with sport management preparation programs (NASPE/NASSM, 1993), and field experiences have become essential components in the professional education and career paths of sport management students (Cuneen & Sidwell, 1993b). Cylkowski (1986) contended that those institutions recognized as having the best curricula in sport management are also notable for excellent field experience programs.

There are typically two components of sport management field experiences for which academic credit is awarded: practica, which constitute part-time placement at external agencies, and internships, which are full-time job commitments similar to management training in industry/enterprise (Bell & Cousins, 1993 Brassie, 1989). Some sport management programs list the practicum as an undergraduate experience and the internship as graduate, although this is not the rule. Other institutions consider the practicum an introductory experience to the profession and the internship as a culminating educational experience. The National Association for Sport and Physical Education (NASPE) and the North American Society for Sport Management (NASSM) have initiated a method of quality control for students and sport management programs by suggesting minimum curricular guidelines for sport management programs. The program standards require that students "shall be able to perform under supervision, management duties assigned by a practicing sport manager. These experiences may be categorized as practica or internships" (NASPE/NASSM, 1993, p. 10).

Practica

According to the NASPE/NASSM *Sport Management Program Standards and Review Protocol* (1993), practica may take a variety of forms.

Some may be extensions of a course while others may be self-contained. Some may be offered for academic credit, while others are not. Typically, these are completed on a part-time basis while involved in other coursework, with less of a time commitment than an internship. Practica are often performed in proximity to the campus and usually involve observing and providing assistance to another professional. They must be directed and evaluated by a qualified faculty member with appropriate supervision by an on-site professional (NASPE/NASSM, 1993, p.10).

Practica are often completed at sites within a reasonable driving radius of the institution so they can be completed while taking other coursework. Policies differ according to individual sport management program, but students are usually eligible for practica only after they have completed a specified number of institution core courses as well as certain major and/or cognate area courses. This benefits students by providing for their readiness in task and observational skills and benefits the sport management program by assuring that only students prepared to specified academic levels are permitted to formally test their proficiencies outside of the classroom. It is common that practica constitute at least three academic credit hours (yielding the appropriate number of clock hours per week). This plan fits the academic schedules of most students, who typically complete their academic series in three-hour courses, and the yielded clock hours constitute an ample introductory opportunity for students to observe and complete assigned tasks at the practicum site. If no academic credit is awarded for successful completion of practica, clock hours are usually determined through consultation with sport management faculty and the selected on-site supervisor.

Internships

The NASPE/NASSM *Sport Management Program Standards and Review Protocol* (1993) describes internship experiences as self-contained for academic credit.

This experience is actual work in a sport management setting subsequent to the junior year in which management practices are applied. Final arrangements for the internship are completed with a member of the faculty. The internship is a full-time (40 hours/week) work experience for a minimum of 400 hours. They must be directed and evaluated by a qualified faculty member with appropriate supervision by an on-site professional (NASPE/NASSM, 1993, p. 10).

The internship is the most common programmatic element of the markedly different sport management preparation programs in the United States (Parkhouse, 1987). Internship experiences are usually scheduled at or near the end of classroom work. This notifies sponsoring organizations that students are familiar with textbook knowledge and in good positions to apply it proficiently. Also completion of internships at the end of classroom education may be advantageous to students if there are possibilities of permanent employment with the sponsoring organization upon field experience completion.

Internships are usually full-time commitments designed to give students pre-professional associations with sponsoring sport organizations (Sidwell, 1984). Because internships are full-time experiences, students generally enroll only for the internship during a particular semester and do not attempt to complete other coursework. Academic credit for internships generally meets institutional criteria for a full-time student. Because interns have full-time employment status at field sites, they may have excellent opportunities to attend meetings, work overtime, travel, or have other developmental experiences. Interns may wish to reduce their commitments to extracurricular activities (such as athletic team participation, student government, work-study programs) that may conflict with field site work.

Field Experience Readiness

Qualified field students have pre-professional experiences through volunteerism, activism, or employment. Experiences such as these enrich students' knowledge making them more able to handle field experience tasks successfully (Young, 1990a). Pre-professional experiences help students build self-satisfaction and demonstrate their willingness to contribute, and their interest and commitment to their chosen careers. If field students have practical experiences in sales/promotions, strategic planning, purchasing, budgeting, or other crucial functions, they are more likely to be hired by sponsoring organizations (Cuneen & Sidwell, 1993b).

Athletics departments on the secondary school and collegiate levels are good places to volunteer as are sales agencies, media, and service and professional groups. Participation or leadership positions in student organizations, and so forth also provide good experiences. Volunteerism indicates maturity, work ethic, professional commitment, and other desirable qualities that sport enterprise personnel consider important in field student search and screening (Cuneen & Sidwell, 1993b).

Sport Management Program Characteristics

Most sport management programs have minimal academic or practical requirements for field experience students. Students must investigate any programmatic minimal requirements as they plan for their field experiences. They should also inquire about any pending changes in current program requirements that may affect their field experience plans. Examples of programmatic requirements for practica and/or internships might be any of the following:
1. Completion of a specified number of academic credit hours.
2. Evidence of academic readiness demonstrated by an acceptable grade point average as determined by program/college or university faculty.
3. Specified number of volunteer or part-time employee hours.
4. Completion of a field experience seminar.
5. Determination of readiness demonstrated in an interview with a field experience review committee comprising faculty and/or practitioners.
6. Delivery of a specified number of recommendation letters from program or college/university faculty attesting to student academic ability, motivation, potential, and so forth.

Criteria such as these attest to student readiness and assure both the sport management program and the sponsoring organization of student proficiency. Many students meet academic criteria for field experiences, but may be unsuitable for field experiences due to maturity level, work ethic, poise, professional composure, and so forth. Report from the Field #2 (see Appendix H) provides an example of an instance in which a student may meet academic criteria, but may not be ready to enter the work environment.

Readiness for Practica

It is best that practicum students have completed the introductory portions of sport management program coursework. This not only satisfies any requisite number of academic hours or other programmatic/institutional criteria, but it also demonstrates a student's academic commitment to sport management as a field of study and intended career. Informal planning for practica, such as investigating possible field sites' schedules and types of positions offered, should begin during students' introductory sport management classes. Students should also consider their intended career direction and path when researching field experiences. The process may entail library work, interviews with professionals in the field, and/or appointments with sport management faculty advisors and college/university counseling or career development officers. Practicum plans should be completed with students' academic advisors and be congruent with plans for internships.

Readiness for Internships

Internships are generally the culminating experiences of sport management preparation. Students are best served and internships are best used as learning strategies when classroom experiences are nearly or actually completed (Sutton, 1989). Therefore, interns should have completed all or most all of their institutional core or general education, sport management major, and related coursework.

A discussion of goals, strategic preparation, pre-entry level qualifications, academic eligibility, and optimum scheduling should be considered relative to the type of internship to be selected (Sidwell, 1992). Students might consider contacting professionals in the field to ascertain their insights concerning the role of interns in their enterprises and the best times and strategies for internship completion. Contacting alumnae/i from the sport management program is also a good method by which to learn about internship readiness; it may also provide initial development opportunities for students. Students should carefully inventory types of internship experiences that will enhance their academic qualifications and solidify career goals. Students should seek advice from persons who can advise them about types of volunteer, part-time employment, and practical experiences crucial to their professional development.

Summary

1. Field experiences are essential links between classroom knowledge and professional practice.
2. Students who have completed field experiences are preferred job candidates.
3. Practicum experiences should be completed after introductory sport management coursework.
4. Internships are generally the culminating experiences of sport management programs.
5. Students need to seek advice from faculty, alumnae/i, practitioners, and career placement officers in planning field experiences.

Suggested Readings

Bell, J. A., & Cousins, J. R. (1993). Professional service through sport management internships. *Journal of Physical Education, Recreation and Dance, 64*(7), 45-52.

Cuneen, J. & Sidwell, M. J. (1993b). Sport management interns: Selection qualifications. *Journal of Physical Education, Recreation and Dance, 64*(1), 91-95.

Cylkowski, G. (1986). A sporting career. *Business Week Careers, 4*(5), 18-23.

Mason, J. G., Higgins, C., & Wilkinson, O. (1981). Sports administration education 15 years later. *Athletic Purchasing and Facilities, 5*, 44-45.

Parks, J. B., & Zanger, B. R. K. (1990). *Sport & fitness management career strategies and professional content.* Champaign, IL: Human Kinetics Books.

Sutton, W. A. (1989). The role of internships in sport management curricula: A model for development. *Journal of Physical Education, Recreation and Dance, 60*(7), 20-24.

Verner, M. E. (1993). Developing professionalism through experiential learning. *Journal of Physical Education, Recreation and Dance, 64*(7), 45-52.

Suggested Activities

1. Investigate the types of field experiences available in a selected sport management program. Are practica required? Are internships required? Can students complete more than one practicum or internship?
2. What are the differences between practica and internships in the selected sport management program? Is the practicum part-time and the internship full-time? How many credit hours of practica or internships are required? Can either be completed while students are taking other classes?
3. When do most students complete their practicum? Their internship (i.e., are they juniors or seniors)?
4. Do most students return to campus for classes after their internships, or are internships generally the last class that students complete?
5. What are the minimal requirements that students must meet in order to complete practica in the selected program? Internships? May students search for field sites before they have met the criteria, or do is formal permission needed to search?

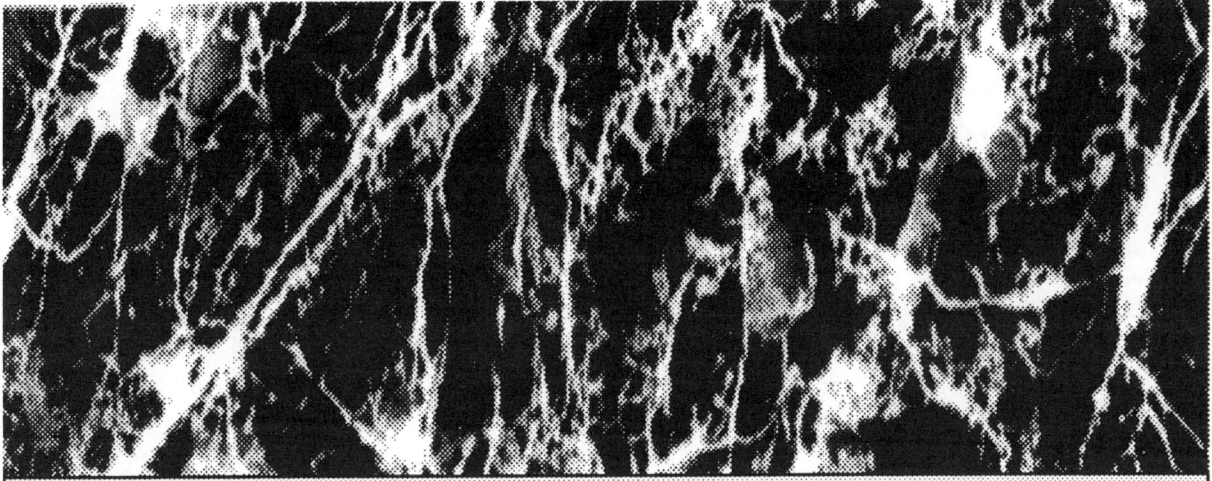

PART II

PLANNING FOR SPORT MANAGEMENT FIELD EXPERIENCES

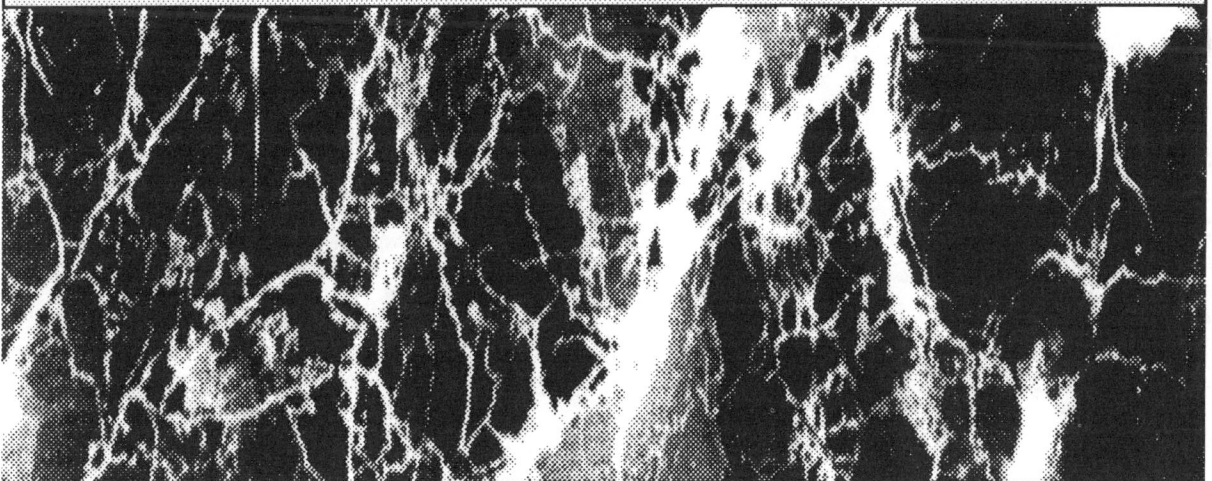

PLANNING FOR SPORT
MANAGEMENT FIELD EXPERIENCES

When students have identified the characteristics of field experiences offered through their sport management programs, they can then begin planning for their own individual experiences. Students have numerous resources to use in their planning and research, such as faculty, alumnae/i, libraries, practitioners, professional associations, publications, and various other sources.

Early Planning

The primary motive in field experience searches should be continued education, although some students, professors, and employers view field experiences as trial periods or management training for potential long-term employment (Parkhouse, 1984). Fieldwork may provide a springboard into a permanent position at a sponsoring organization or subsidiary (Parks & Zanger, 1990). The relationship of field experiences and employment became clear when Parks (1991) found that personal contacts, such as those made during field experiences, played major roles in first job attainment for sport management students. For these practical reasons, students need to plan carefully for their field experiences from the beginning of their academic preparation.

Field experiences should be compatible with specific career objectives (Parkhouse, 1984). Students should compile lists of career aspirations, and 3-, 5-, and 10-year goals. Field experiences should be related directly to short-term goals and be congruent with long-term career goals in order to most beneficial.

Students can become familiar with any pre-entry and career path phenomena associated with certain types of sport managerial positions by planning field experiences. For both practica and internships, students should study the types of organizations to which they will be applying. Students should research all details of an organization's field experience policies, procedures, functions, and so forth, by consulting with faculty, alumnae/i, and practitioners. According to the *NAGWS Guide for Internships: Climbing the Ladder* (National Association for Girls and Women in Sport, 1991), students should learn as much as possible about potential sites by asking questions of professionals at sites that match students' interests. NAGWS suggested several core questions for students to ask:
1. What types of projects are available for field students?
2. What types of projects have students worked on recently? What were their responsibilities?
3. Can names and addresses of past field students be provided?
4. Who would have primary responsibility for field students?

5. What specific skills are expected of field students? Are there any proficiencies required for certain computer hardware and software? Is there any special training offered that can enhance students' skills, résumés, and marketability as a result of learning them?

6. What types of "fill-in" jobs will be expected? Are field students required to file, type, proof read, and so forth?

7. What is the duration of the experience? What are the start and end dates? Is the time flexible? What are the application deadlines?

8. What are the work hours? Five days a week? Eight hours per day?

9. What kind of credit is available? (Most sponsoring organizations will work individually with students and sport management programs in extending academic credit for both practica and internships.)

10. Is remuneration provided?

Sometimes, students can learn much about organizations merely by observing them. The Field and International Study Program of the New York State College of Human Ecology (Cornell University, 1986) offered an inductive skills-building exercise in ways to gather data about field sites. It will be necessary to make site visits in order to complete the exercise. Some questions that students might ask based upon the Field and International Study Program suggestions include:

1. What are the objectives of the data-gathering research? What should one hope to learn?

2. How can objectives be accomplished? What strategies can be used to achieve objectives? For instance, if one wishes to learn about the attitudes of personnel in the ticket office toward special needs of spectators, what are the most likely sources of information?

3. What are the issues one should consider? How do the issues relate to learning objectives?

4. What does the physical setting look and sound like? Consider the rooms, furnishings, noises, color etc. and other details.

5. Who are the people observed and what are their ages and genders? How are they dressed? How many people are around and does the number change over time? What groupings can be observed?

6. What principal activities are occurring? How are people interacting? Can different roles be observed? What are the important elements?

7. What are the speculations about has been observed?

Many organizations cooperate with students who wish to learn more about work and careers. Students should call any organization in which they are interested and ask permission to observe the site during typical work hours. If students are unobtrusive, they are usually given special attention and invited back to observe again.

Annual Reports

An especially good way to learn specific facts about a sponsoring organization is to study the organization annual report. Annual reports of larger organizations are usually available in college/university libraries, but several North American companies will distrib ute their reports to any individual who requests one. Reports provide comprehensive information related to operations, profits, losses, mission, products, services, sales, earnings, key personnel, and significant events (Career Planning and Placement Services, 1993). The type of information contained in annual reports will not only help students learn about characteristics of an organization, but it also will help in their preparation if they are invited to interview for a field position. Table 1 provides a guide to the typical information contained in annual reports.

Table 1. Characteristics Of Annual Reports

- **Letter from the Chair:** Chief Executive's statement explaining why the organization performed as it did in the previous year

- **Assets:** What the company owns

- **Liabilities:** What the company owes

- **Balance Sheet:** A list of assets and liabilities

- **Auditor's Report:** Written by an independent Certified Public Accountant to indicate if principles in preparing the report conformed to acceptable accounting standards

- **Current Liabilities:** Debts due in a year and paid from current assets

- **Net Working Capital:** Money used for day-to-day operations

- **Stockholder's Equity:** Difference between total assets and liabilities; presumed value of what stockholders own

- **Income Statement:** Financial report showing the amount of money made or lost in previous year

- **Net Sales:** Sales activity/charges in company holdings

- **Debt-To-Equity Ratio:** Difference between long-term liabilities and stockholder's equity

Note: The information in this table is from *Career Search,* (page 52) by Career Planning and Placement Services, 1993. Bowling Green, OH: Bowling Green State University. Copyright © 1993 by Bowling Green State University. Adapted by permission.

Unique Characteristics of Field Sites

There are several considerations related to timing and the types of experiences students will have in the field. Students should be familiar with any unique characteristics of certain enterprises and plan their field experience semesters according to the schedule of the organization. Certain organizations offer field experiences only during summer or other specified times such as during peaks in their marketing or business traffic. Timing of the field experience should follow the organization's schedule in those cases, especially if there is a particular enterprise with which a student wishes to complete the field experience. For instance, events management groups may hire field students only during the events themselves and not during the planning stages. They may wish to use field students for functions, such as crowd management, ticket dispersion, hospitality, or media information, rather than for planning-type activities such as advertising sales, sponsorship, or itinerary plans. Or sporting goods retailers may gear up for high-traffic spring and summer seasons beginning late in the previous fall and early winter. Ordering, stocking, cataloging, planning for inventory display and point-of-purchase advertising, and media advertising strategies are determined long before consumers have access to traditional spring and summer sports products. Therefore, a rich field experience in retail sales may be better available before a traditionally busy season than during the actual sales campaign.

Although it is generally not considered so by the general public, summer may be the busiest season for collegiate departments of athletics. During summer, ads are sold for fall sports programs, media guides are prepared for the fall and conceptualized for the winter sports, and decisions are made concerning budgets, travel, and scheduling for subsequent operating years. If students wish to be involved in tasks such as these, it might be sound for them to do their collegiate athletics field work in summer in order to learn the most about marketing and promotions, sports information, or budget. Students need to plan academic schedules and make curricular decisions early while considering the characteristics of sponsoring organizations.

Field Experience Quality

Field experiences should enable students to grow personally and professionally. The types of experiences provided to students by organizations play key roles in student development and add to the success of experiential education. "Reports From the Field #5 and 6" (see Appendix H) were written by two former interns who found their field experiences to be enriching from academic, professional, and personal perspectives. To secure enriching experiences, students must investigate all aspects of potential sponsoring organizations, determine if there are any differences in field experience tasks based on student qualifications that are unrelated to professional dimensions, investigate the experiences of previous field experience students, and examine the contributing roles of regular employees of the sponsoring organization. Students should determine if field students are directed toward staff-type functions such as human resources and research, or if they are given functional-type assignments, such as sales and production, where they learn about corporate "bottom lines."

Students should have opportunities to interact with personnel in other departments and other organizations. Volunteering at the sponsoring organization is a good way to meet persons with similar interests and goals, provided it does not detract from regular assignments or cause time management problems. Accepting additional assignments and branching out enhance academic and practical preparation.

The subject matter inherent in sport management is professional, and application is extremely important; field experiences are more purposeful when students are supervised closely by on-site practitioners and faculty representing the training program (Parkhouse, 1984). Sponsoring organizations must willing to let students have access to their faculty supervisors during working hours and accommodate faculty supervisors if they are able to visit the worksite. Faculty supervisors contribute to field education in numerous ways. An overview of the types of contributions made by faculty supervisors is provided in Appendix H-1.

Sponsoring Organizations

Many companies oversee career advancement of key individuals by providing for internal development, including rotational assignments, mentoring and training, and executive development programs (United States Department of Labor, 1991). Those functions enhance academic or work-related credentials and goal achievement (Young, 1990b). It is very important to determine the status of previous field students and regular employees at the sponsoring organization. Organizations sometimes discriminate consciously or unconsciously based on gender, race, religion, and numerous other social variables. For example, if female field students and current female employees are assigned staff-type tasks while males are assigned to line functions, then the quality of experiences available to females at the sponsoring organization may be limited severely. It is important to determine if all employees and field students benefit from the same types of developmental experiences.

The Search for Sites

Sponsoring organizations are cooperating associates of colleges/universities, and students' faculty advisors or sport management program field experience coordinators/ directors may assist students in site selection. Field experience sites should be selected based on the best experiences available related to amount and type of work. Although they are important considerations, proximity to available lodging or home, remuneration, ease of selection, and prestige of the sponsoring organization should not be prioritized. Field experience sites should be selected based on the breadth and depth of opportunities to function professionally in the organization (Sidwell, 1984). For example, if students have paid internships assisting in group ticket distribution for a major league baseball club near their homes or can complete nonpaid internships assisting in group ticket sales and telemarketing for a semi-professional baseball team far away from home, the latter might be considered more seriously because of the types of experiences offered. There may be value in completing even menial tasks during field experiences if students can still observe and interact with professionals (Bell & Cousins, 1993), but they might have more opportunity to use their acquired skills and learn more in a rich, contributing experience for a small enterprise than in an "envelope stuffing" experience for a defending World Series championship team.

The *NAGWS Guide for Internships: Climbing the Ladder* (NAGWS, 1991) suggests several variables to analyze in site selection. Students may wish to consider the following in their site searches:

1. The internship should provide pertinent/practical experiences in at least one major project every three months such as a publication, budget review, brochure revision/ development, event management, research.
2. The organizational structure should allow one person to supervise, guide and mentor the intern.
3. Opportunities to work with others within the organization should be provided. Interns should be able to observe committee meetings, attend important meetings, and learn more about themselves.
4. Experiences should allow students to pursue their interests.
5. Appropriate time spans should be considered. Summer experiences are problematic if they are only six weeks long; it may take longer to become familiar with organizational complexity, or be responsible for a project from start to finish.

Some sport management programs forbid students to select sites that have never sponsored field experience students, although most programs are willing to work with organizations to implement experiential education strategies. Appendices H-3 and H-4 relate successful stories of organizations that worked with sport management programs and students to inaugurate field experience programs.

Typical Field Experience Venues

The sport enterprises are enthusiastic about sponsoring field experience students. Field experiences provide cost-effective personnel and training avenues for industry (Ciofalo, 1992). Firms also view field students as creative and energetic internal resources who contribute to high standards and generate interest (Brightman, 1989). Field students help employers in accomplishing projects not otherwise possible due to economic resources (Stanton & Ali, 1987) and provide fresh ideas where there is insufficient staff (Patton & Dial, 1988). Field experience programs also give sponsoring agencies the opportunity to support higher education by providing fundamental work experiences to students (Hollingsworth, 1990). Sport enterprises expect applications from field students on a semester or yearly basis, and numerous agencies employ designated personnel in human resources whose sole assignment is related to field-student screening. Some organizations pre-employ so many field students that there are special seminars held for those students who will be applying and seminars that continue after appointment for those who have been selected.

There are numerous placement venues for field experiences. College and university athletics departments have availabilities in the business office, sports information office, ticket office, marketing and promotions, scheduling, contest management, compliance, academic counseling, booster or donor organizations, and other divisions. Minor and major league professional sport franchises also provide opportunities in most of the same areas, as do Special Olympics, Canadian, United States or International Olympics, individual state-level games, and other competitions planned for special age or interest groups. Offices of collegiate sports conferences usually offer one or more field experience positions per semester. But sport enterprise involves more than merely collegiate athletics, professional franchises, and special events. Local, regional, national, and brokerage media support field experiences for students not only from sport management, but also from journalism, business, mass or interpersonal communications, public relations, and marketing. Local sporting events, such as amateur tournaments, or those professional tournaments sanctioned by a national, governing body, such as the Ladies Professional Golf Association (LPGA), the Professional Golf Association (PGA), or the United States Tennis Association (USTA), offer excellent opportunities for learning. Coaches' associations, conference offices, and club/federation offices are also excellent field sites. Fundraising events, such as those tournaments and games sponsored locally to raise capital for recreation complexes, are numerous, and committees usually welcome and use the skills of field experience students well. Sporting goods retail and wholesale outlets are excellent sites to investigate. State or provincial games sponsored for secondary school and adult amateur athletes have become popular across the United States and Canada, and most organizing committees offer positions to several field experience students per year. Public or private golf course management organizations or sports complex management groups generally offer various field experiences. Clubs and resorts have several multipurpose field positions available. Sports marketing, player/talent agencies, and events promotions organizations accept field experience students, as do the sponsorship departments of industries, corporate fitness management, and novelty businesses such as batting-cage franchises, local, state, national, or international sports halls of fame, concessionaires, mail-order merchants, licensing offices, sports publishers, advertising agencies and market research firms, and myriad other enterprises related to sport.

Strategies for Obtaining Field Experiences

Generally, students are responsible for searching and screening their own field experience positions, but some sport management programs require students to work in concert with faculty during the search and screening process. Table 2 shows some advantages to student self- searches; Table 3 shows some disadvantages.

Search and screening procedures require careful consideration, initiative, and planning (Sidwell, 1984). Securing field experience positions is similar to securing regular employment (Cuneen & Sidwell, 1993b), and field experience applicants should approach field experience employers in the same ways they would approach a full-time employer (Wurfel, 1985). The field experience search and screening process provides to students a learning experience in itself (Brown, 1992).

Networks

A viable strategy for obtaining field experiences is through networks, groups of people bonded by like interests and similar goals that are social or professional. Professionals interact with others on a variety of levels. Students can learn of field positions or obtain field experiences through "gatekeepers," those persons in the network who define "who talks to whom." Family friends or colleagues who know the niece of the director of player personnel for a professional soccer team, a friend's father who is director of sports medicine for the provincial youth sport foundation, or an aunt who has invested in a sports

Table 2. Advantages Of Students' Self-Search For Field Experiences

- It is part of the motivation process.
- It helps prepare students for the actual entry-level job search.
- Students may have opportunities to help with development of objectives by the sponsoring organization.
- Students may learn more about the sponsoring organization through library work and other data-gathering.
- It may enable students to discuss the field site and experience with previous students.
- It may enable students to evaluate their own skills relative to the sponsoring organization needs.
- Students may be able to negotiate remuneration.

radio brokerage enterprise all represent gatekeepers in social or professional networks. Several students obtain field experiences through knowing previous field students, classmates, family, and friends and faculty.

Personal contacts are an important source of information in choosing occupations (Bolles, 1987) and obtaining first jobs (Parks, 1991). Contacts become even more important as parts of the vast networks of relationships and interrelationships (Parks & Zanger, 1990). And, despite claims of cultural or familial nepotism, it is wise rather than unethical to use contacts in securing field experiences. Naturally, "knowing somebody" is not the sole criterion in landing field experiences. Gatekeepers have power to arrange introductions or interviews for potential field students, but credentials, recommendations, and professional demeanor during the hiring process are essential for sealing the offer.

Institutional Arrangements/Special Circumstance Field Experiences

Some institutions have established formal or informal contracts with outside enterprises to provide some or all of their field students. Contractual agreements between institutions and sponsoring organizations are becoming more common; some agreements prohibit agencies from hiring field students from competing sport management programs. The sponsoring organization usually pays a fee to the university that is remunerated solely to the university. For example, University X is situated in a city where a minor league baseball team competes. The ball club accepts three of their field experience students per semester. For providing the club with three pre-entry level employees each semester, the

Table 3. Disadvantages Of Students' Self-Search For Field Experiences

- Search may be based on convenience rather than experiences available.

- Search may not be thorough.

- Search may be unduly influenced by other people (e. g., friends, relatives) or variables such as fame or appearance of the sponsoring organization

- Field experience site may be selected based on remuneration regardless of types of experiences available.

- Expectations may be unrealistic.

- Students may not judge field experience living expenses accurately.

club will remunerate to University X a specified sum of money per year. The university has the option to share a portion of the amount with field students, or field students may receive a portion from the organization. Some agreements between institutions and sponsoring organizations may provide tuition and fees for students during their field semesters. Sometimes, these field experiences are not available to all sport management majors within the particular program, but are available only to students who have met certain criteria. Those who do not meet criteria are not permitted to interview or compete for the field positions.

Sometimes, there are "unannounced" field experiences available. They are established through mutual agreement between sport management faculty and enterprise professionals who have interacted in their personal or career paths. These field experiences are also unavailable to all students in the sport management program but rather are reserved for those students of special standing determined at the sole discretion of the faculty.

Some organizations have had success with field students from specific institutions and prefer to use students only from those programs. Sites request field students one or more times per year and may not even interview students from other programs. Other organizations have provided specialized equipment or supplies (such as computerized ticket hardware and software) to programs that train students in their use. The site then accepts only those students who demonstrate specific task proficiencies. Still other organizations, such as some collegiate athletics conference offices, only offer field experiences to students from their member institutions on a rotating basis. Potential field students should consult with the field experience coordinator or faculty to investigate those agencies that may offer special circumstance field experiences.

Sport Management Program Sources

Students need to become familiar with any sport management program materials that will assist them in field experience site search and screening. Most programs have field experience directories or files for students to use in their searches for field site searches. Computerized files are the most efficient systems (Sidwell, 1984) because they can be coded and cross-filed. Then, information can be found in various ways, such as by academic program concentration (marketing, sales, information, management, etc.), organization type (fitness center, professional team, aquatics management, etc.), location (country, city, state or province, region, etc.), and paid/unpaid status. Files are updated regularly so they may be the most currently available knowledge about site and site supervisor information. They are usually stored in centrally located facilities that offer extended hours so students have easy access to them.

Some sport management programs also require field students to prepare portfolios or summaries on their sponsoring organizations that describe types of work performed while with the organization, the quality of work assignments they received, and enrichment experiences. The documents are kept on file so future students can examine them and determine if the site and experiences are of the type they would consider.

Cooperative Programs

Campus career development or cooperative education (co-op) programs are also good sources of field site information. Many institutions offer career planning and placement services for their students, and many offices assist not only in regular employment processes but also in field experience pre-career development. Students should investigate services such as individual counseling, on-campus interview programs, interview training, referral systems, and vacancy listings. Generally, minimal fees are assessed to students for these services. Co-op offices receive requests for field students from a multitude of enterprises and industries. Some campus co-op offices have the staff to seek field sites for students according to their own requests, areas of interests, and desired tasks. Appropriate employers then interview prospective co-op students and select those who are best suited for particular openings. Co-op students are usually paid the prevailing wages for persons with their types of backgrounds and experiences. Duration of experiences are determined by the co-op office and the sponsoring organization, but time in the field usually meets or exceeds students' academic criteria. Contractual arrangements vary between co-op offices, but most require on-site supervision, regular communication between the enterprise and the co-op office, and other protective measures. Students using co-op offices should reconcile any co-op office policies with sport management major program policies. Usually, both the sport management programs and the co-op offices have congruent missions, but some details may require clarification pertaining to supervision, academic requirements, and so forth. For sport management students who need to be supervised by their own faculty, co-op programs should be willing to share or concede supervisory aspects.

Directories

Several directories exist for sport enterprises. Many sport management programs subscribe to publications containing contact names, addresses, and in some cases, descriptions of various sport enterprises. However, an interesting phenomenon related to sport careers is the tendency of leadership to change frequently; therefore, names of contacts listed in the publications are subject to quick change. Perhaps the best usage of these directories would be to secure the telephone numbers and check the names of the current personnel. Professional periodicals or trade journals from various fields of specialization are excellent sources of vacancy information. The *NAGWS Guide to Internships: Climbing the Corporate Ladder* (NAGWS, 1991) lists several internship programs available within the sport enterprises.

Field Experience Placement Services

Field experiences are common to so many academic programs that national level field experience/apprentice services have been created to assist both students and enterprise/industry. The services are associated with networks across the United States and Canada, and they publish field experience listings two or more times per year. Field sites with available pre-entry positions are charged nominal fees to have their position announcements or advertising published in the listings. Some services also assist enterprise in developing field experience programs and recruit appropriate field students on an ongoing or limited referral basis. Occasionally, the services provide supervision to field students, eliminating that criterion for field site personnel. For most services such as these, students are charged a subscription fee for the lists, and fees are assessed to the student based on search, acceptance, and so forth. Students should reconcile any such services' policies with their sport management program policies. Some programs may require direct supervision by on-site personnel from the sponsoring organization rather than from placement service personnel. Details should be defined at the beginning of the process.

Professional Conventions, Conferences, and Trade Shows

Annual conventions, conferences, and trade shows are also good sources of field experience vacancies. There are hundreds of associations, alliances, and professional affiliations related to sport enterprise that meet annually or more often. Some common conferences are: (a) the Winter Baseball Meetings, (b) Women's Sports Foundation (WSF), (c) National Collegiate Athletics Association (NCAA), (d) National Association of Intercollegiate Athletics (NAIA), (e) North American Society for Sport Management, (f) Amateur Athletic Union (AAU), (g) Canadian Intra-University Athletics, (h) National Association of Broadcasters (NAB), (i) National Association of Collegiate Directors of Athletics, (j) American Alliance of Health, Physical Education, Recreation and Dance (AAHPERD), (k) Canadian Association for Health, Physical Education, Recreation and Dance (CAHPERD), and various state and provincial broadcasting, and print media conferences. Students should obtain information relative to specific, professional organizations or associations whose members might be potential contacts for field experience information.

Private/Public/Municipal Industries

Students should investigate the conference schedules for marina, resort, or club managers, sporting goods retailers and wholesalers, and industries or corporations that have made heavy commitments to sports sponsorships. Professional meetings for advertising agencies, arena and events managers, recreation complex managers, public parks programs, campus recreation directors, and so forth. are also good possibilities. The concept of sport and leisure entertainment is so broadly based that opportunities for sport management field experiences exist by the thousands. Several United States cities, such as Indianapolis, Indiana; North Mankato, Minnesota; and Blue Springs, Missouri, have made commitments to bring all types of sporting events to their cities as a strategy for boosting commerce (Crookham, 1993). Civic offices in cities such as these can offer excellent experiences.

Duration of Sport Management Field Experiences

At least one field experience, usually the internship, should be a full-time assignment and constitute a full-time academic load. Sport management programs usually make field experiences available each semester or quarter, including summers, although individual institutional size and academic calendar can restrain or support field experience program size and characteristics (Gryski, Johnson, & O'Toole, 1992). Smaller programs may lack faculty and resources necessary for supervision during certain semesters.

Field experiences constitute genuine academic classes, and the duration of the "class" should be congruent with other courses offered by the program and institution in a given semester or quarter. As much as possible, field experiences begin and end according to faculty contracts within an officially designated university session (Sidwell, 1992). Sometimes, field experiences will have to be arranged at the convenience or need of sponsoring organizations, and time frames of experiences will have to be individually prescribed. In these cases, students will have to adhere to appropriate time spans defined by the sport management faculty and/or field experience coordinator/director.

Individual institutions have unique criteria for determining ways of reconciling academic semester or quarter credit hours to actual clock hours. For field experiences, academic credit hours are usually determined by matching site or sponsoring organization needs with the amount of quality time field experience students can commit (Sidwell, 1992). For example, for each credit hour to be awarded upon completion of the field experience, a student may participate in field activities a minimum of 3 clock hours per week for one semester. Table 4 outlines an example of ways in which academic and clock hours can be reconciled using a 1-credit, 3-clock-hour basis. Field experience students should consult with academic advisors and field experience coordinators to learn academic credit patterns of their programs and institutions.

Table 4. Credit Hour/Clock Hour Reconciliation For 15-Week Field Experience

Credit Hours for Field Experience (per semester)	Clock Hours at Organization (per week)	(Total)
1	3	45
2	6	90
3	9	135
4	12	180
5	15	225

Financial Considerations

Students should ascertain field experience costs in their planning. Individual institutions and programs implement different charges and payment standards related to experiential education. Field experience semester(s) can potentially be more expensive than traditional semesters, even exceeding those in which expensive textbook costs are incurred. However, students who believe the field experience to be a financial hardship might be wise to heed Taylor's (1988) suggestion that the advantages to the student prompted by the internship make the time and effort investment cost effective in the long term.

Because there are so many opportunities to complete practica on campuses, finances may not be affected as drastically as when practica are completed off campus. If practica are completed in proximity to campus but outside of walking or biking distance, public or personal transportation must be arranged. For internships, and those practica completed far off campus, students should plan to pay rent for their lodging, securities, insurance and other renting/owning deposits, food costs, transportation to the field site both for relocation and daily commuting, and other self-support.

Appropriate tuition and other fees are assessed to students receiving academic credit for their field experiences. Some institutions waive or reduce fees for sport management field students, student teachers, accounting or journalism apprentices, and others who are completing the experiential components of their programs. In some states and provinces, institutions may not assess all fees to students who reside outside a critical commuting radius from their main campuses. Some institutions will charge only partial fees if students will waive rights to attend "fee-funded events," such as athletics contests, concerts, exhibits and plays or will not be using specially funded services such as health care. Field students need to investigate the fee policies at their individual institutions.

Regular tuition is usually paid because field students have access to institutional services, such as the library, mainframe or micro-computer facilities, media laboratories, academic or personal counseling, health services, and career counseling. Field students are duly enrolled and receiving academic credit for completing field experiences, thus are entitled to use any facility or service as if they were completing classes on campus. Many field students return to campus to gather library information or use campus computer services to complete a field assignment for their sponsoring organizations. Because field experiences are bona fide classes, supervising faculty are available, just as in other major classes, to consult with students concerning professional projects and tasks assigned by the site supervisor.

Some institutions assess a field experience fee. Fees of this sort are common in student teaching, media internships, business or technology out-reach, or cooperative experiences and various other programs. The fee covers expenses incurred in phone and fax communications, postal services, or supervisor travel. Fees also offset institutional costs for field experience academic materials, such as procedural forms and weekly reports or logs.

Site Location

There are a number of variables for students to consider related to site selection and proximity to campus. Tables 5 and 6 outline some of the frequently important considerations.

Proximity to campus will enable students to have access to university health services, library, mainframe and/or micro-computer facilities, faculty, and campus events, etc. But, if field experiences are completed in distant metropolitan areas, students may have access to large public libraries and other supports. Students who have to complete field experiences near their homes for financial reasons may be limited in their choices of sites.

Some institutions define a critical driving radius for external visits that limits the number of site visits by faculty. When sites are outside the radius, field students and supervising faculty communicate via telephone, e-mail, fax, and post.

Table 5. Field Experience Supervision: Student Placement Close To Campus

---

• One or more visits to site by the faculty supervisor

• Opportunity to attend professional development seminars held for field experience s t u - dents

• Opportunities to attend campus or community activities

• Opportunities for regularly scheduled meetings with faculty supervisor

• Access to college/university services, such as health, library, computer, social

Table 6. Field Experience Supervision: Student Placement At Long Distance From Campus

• Few or no site visits by faculty supervisor

• Telephone, fax, voice-mail, or e-mail correspondence with faculty supervisor

• Final evaluations based on correspondence

• No opportunities for regularly scheduled meetings with faculty supervisor

• No opportunity to attend professional development seminars held for field experience students

• No access to college/university services, such as health, library, computer, social

Outside Commitments

Some field experience sites may forbid outside commitments. Others may allow outside commitments for practicum students but not for interns. Students should check the policies of sponsoring organizations. Practica (depending on number of hours) can usually be completed while taking other academic course work or while students have extracurricular commitments, such as athletics team competition, music or drama participation, sorority or fraternity activities, or community volunteerism. Commitments such as part-time work or self-supporting jobs are also possible, but too many commitments may limit students' opportunities for overtime work at the practicum site. Or commitments might interfere with students' concentration while they are completing tasks. Some sport management programs permit students to have outside commitments during internships, but the importance of internships as full-time experiences is crucial enough to warrant that most programs recommend that the sole commitments of the students should be with the field experience.

Remuneration for Field Experiences

Numerous organizations offer salary, stipends, honoraria, or other forms of payment for field experience students. Remuneration is generally negotiated between field experience students and the sponsoring organizations. Practica students are typically not paid, although some field sites consider practicum students to be part-time employees and arrange some form of payment. Many students locate paid summer employment that meets field experience program guidelines, and they can complete the field experience "on the job."

Some sport management programs require that students locate paid field experiences. Other programs stipulate that field experience students must be volunteers at sponsoring organizations so they can be safeguarded by their faculty during the experiences.

Acceptance of Field Experience

A confirmation should be sent to a sponsoring organization when a student accepts a field experience. Some sport management programs have standardized acceptance forms available for student use, but letters of acceptance authored by students are more common. Some sponsoring organizations issue legally binding contracts to their field students.

Confirmation documents or letters constitute learning agreements and denote an obligation to the organization. When organizations accept field students, their search and screening process halts; their "student staffs" are full, and the organization denies the subsequent applications of other interested students. Upon acceptance, there should be no additional search or screening for field experiences by the student. To seek or accept another position constitutes unethical behavior and will reflect badly on the student, the sport management program, and the institution.

Summary

1. Field experiences constitute continued education.
2. Gathering information on sites, supervision, functions, timing, and extra cost is the most crucial element of field experience searches.
3. Students should use every available source in field experience searches, such as sport management program files, directories, networks, alumnae/i, field experience placement services, cooperative education offices, and professional affiliations, and meetings.
4. Both sites and institutions have specific criteria that field experience students must meet.
5. Potential field experience students need to ascertain exactly what functions they will be expected to perform at sponsoring organizations before they accept a field experience.

Suggested Readings

Cornell University. (1986). *Learning from field experience: An ethnographic approach to experiential education.* Ithaca, NY: New York State College of Human Ecology.

National Association for Girls and Women in Sport. (1991). *NAGWS guide to internships: Climbing the corporate ladder.* Reston, VA: American Alliance for Health, Physical Education, Recreation and Dance.

Stanton, T., & Ali, K. (1987). *The experienced hand: A student manual for making the most of an internship.* Cranston, RI: Carroll Press Publishers.

United States Department of Labor. (1991). *A report on the glass ceiling initiative.* Washington, DC: U. S. Government Printing Office.

Wurfel, W. W. (1985). Well-nurtured interns can reap benefits and bring rewards. *Public Relations Journal, 41*(4), 37.

Young, D. (1990b). Mentoring and networking: Perceptions by athletic administrators. *Journal of Sport Management, 4*(2), 71-79.

Suggested Activities

1. Define specific aspirations for a career in sport management. List 3-, 5-, and 10-year goals. Are the career aspirations realistic? Can the goals be achieved in the appropriate time spans? What professional can you ask about your aspirations and goals?

2. Determine if the specific sport management program maintains files of those sites where your predecessors completed their field experiences. Are the files computerized? Are specific skills needed in order to access the files from the computer? Are other materials such as public relations packets available?

3. Determine if there are any arranged or special circumstance field experiences available through the sport management program. How do students qualify for them? Are special skills needed? Special experiences? How do students acquire any special skills or experiences in order to qualify?

4. List those organizations that are congruent with career aspirations and goals. How should one contact field students who have been there? Is there a sport management alumnae/i organization? Can any member of the alumnae/i organization assist students in securing a field experience at any of the organizations?

5. Locate a listing of professional affiliations/associations for persons in a specific field. How can students find out the more important ones to join?

6. Compile a list of all costs that might be incurred during any field experience terms(s). Is it affordable to relocate? What alternatives do students have related to financing the field experience?

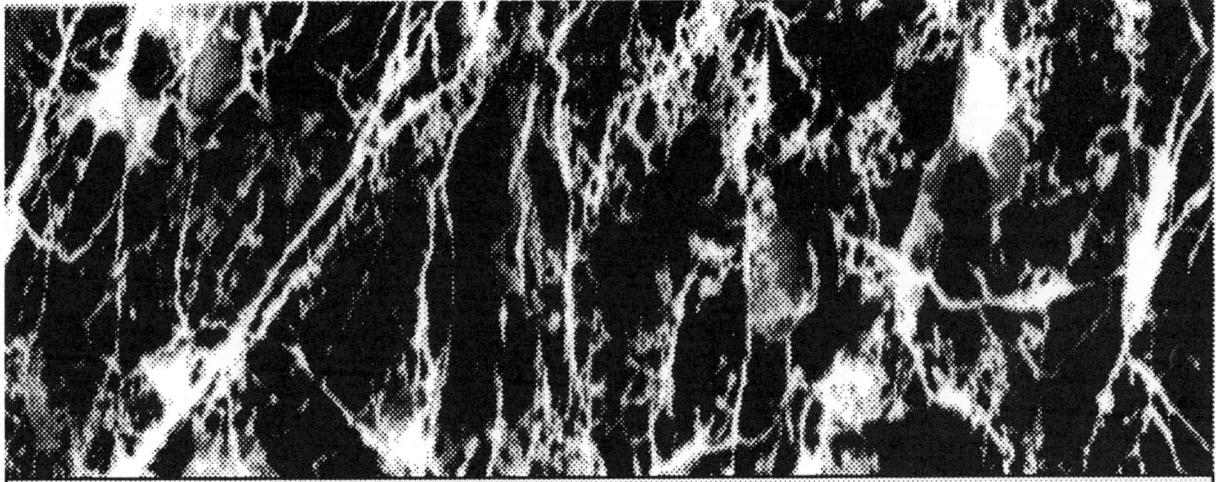

PART III

PLANNING, PREPARING, AND PRESENTING CREDENTIALS FOR FIELD EXPERIENCES

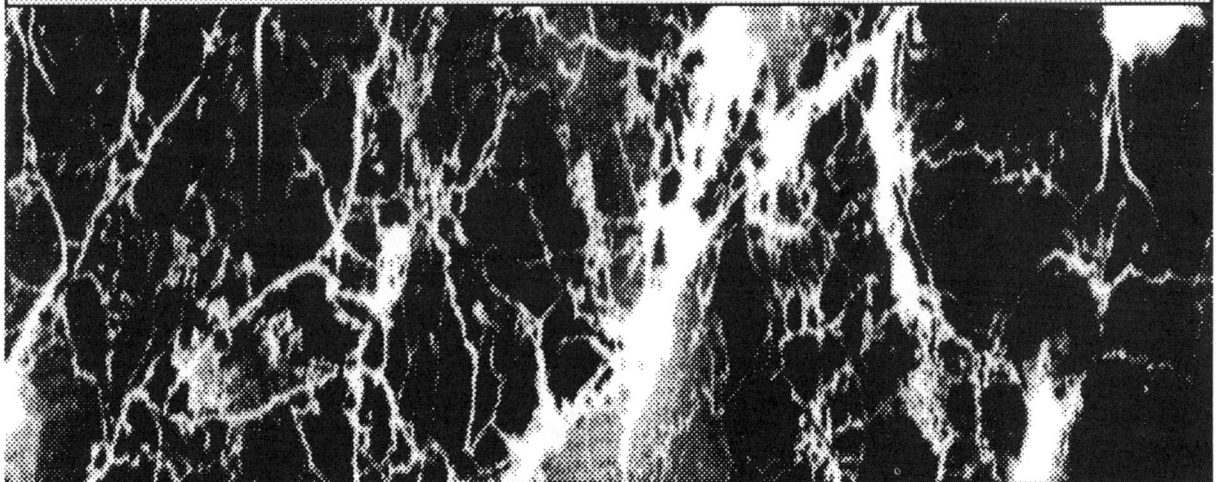

PLANNING, PREPARING, AND PRESENTING CREDENTIALS FOR FIELD EXPERIENCES

As students are researching field sites, they may also want to start preparing their field experience credentials. Credentials constitute substantial statements of who the students are, what they have accomplished, and what they wish to accomplish. As students gather information about potential sites and sponsoring organizations' needs, they may wish to compile lists of their own qualifications that will meet the organizations' requisites.

Campus placement offices are the most appropriate sources for information on credentials preparation. Sometimes, career specialists are assigned to certain fields of study and can offer assistance in specific credentials preparation for certain industries and enterprises. Usually, there are no consultation fees; some offices offer to print résumés for students, charging only nominal fees to cover printing cost. Most offices will provide consultation and allow candidates to have materials printed elsewhere. It is crucial for students to investigate the options available to them on campus when preparing credentials.

Résumés

Paper credentials are the initial and occasionally the only vehicle by which field experience applicants are judged and selected, and are crucial in obtaining quality field experiences (Cuneen & Sidwell, 1993b). Résumés are comprehensive summaries of students' academic, professional, and personal accomplishments that make focused statements about field experience candidates. Résumés should be concise; some agencies will not examine student résumés over one page in length. Résumés must be professional and contain complete, accurate information related to the types of field experiences for which students are applying. Résumés should be written in positive, action-oriented language that conveys what students can contribute to sponsoring organizations. Examples of key, action-oriented words that students might use to describe themselves (Career Planning and Placement Services, 1993) are listed in Table 7.

There are no firm rules guiding résumé contents or formats. Numerous résumé software packages are available commercially. They guide students through résumé preparation by prompting appropriate questions on vital information and formatting the contents for the user. Professional credentials consultants are also available in most cities. They have currently useful knowledge about competencies generic to certain fields, and students may wish to employ such services for their initial credentials preparation.

Some organizations subscribe to a uniform credentials format. In their research of potential field sites, students need to discern any standardized application procedures. If an agency is accustomed to screening candidates who apply using a certain résumé format, then even the most suitable candidates may not have their credentials reviewed if they are not prepared according to organization guidelines.

Table 7. Action Words

Adjectives	Nouns	Verbs
Accelerated	Ability	Achieved
Capable	Ambition	Administered
Conscientious	Confidence	Analyzed
Detailed	Diversity	Budgeted
Determined	Economy	Clarified
Distinctive	Excellence	Conducted
Effective	Harmony	Coordinated
Efficient	Imagination	Designed
Goal Oriented	Ingenuity	Directed
Helpful	Judgment	Expanded
Lasting	Merit	Financed
Mutual	Progress	Generated
Notable	Recognition	Implemented
Proficient	Stability	Initiated
Reasonable	Success	Integrated
Responsible		Justified
Substantial		Keynoted
Superior		Launched
Useful		Managed
Vital		Marketed
		Negotiated
		Piloted
		Researched
		Solved
		Supervised
		Transformed
		Unified
		Verified

Note: The information in this table is from *Career Search*, (page 41) by Career Planning and Placement Services, 1993. Bowling Green, OH: Bowling Green State University. Copyright © 1993 by Bowling Green State University. Adapted by permission.

Resume Formats

Students need to design their résumés to describe their skills and experiences in the best possible way. The formatting of the résumé document is important in highlighting students' qualities. The more common formats are:
   1. Chronological: Arranged in reverse chronological order, emphasizes job titles and organizations with a description of responsibilities and duties included.

2. Functional: Accents accomplishments and strengths leaving job titles and work history in subordinate position.
3. Combined: Emphasizes skills first followed by employment history.

The chronological résumé style highlights continuity and career growth; the functional style offers more flexibility and reduces repetition of job assignments; and the combined format is best used when students need to show their responsibility and potential but have employment histories not directly related to jobs (Career Planning and Placement Services, 1993). Career planning and placement offices usually have several different examples of résumés on file, and students should examine them to choose the style that best fits their purposes. Generally, résumés contain the following information about candidates:

1. Full name, address (temporary and permanent), telephone, fax or e-mail numbers.
2. Statement of field experience objective.
3. Academic preparation and dates (or anticipated dates) of graduation.
4. Experience and work history.
5. Related activities and interests.
6. References.

Statement of Field Experience Goal

The field experience goal or statement of field experience objective is often the most difficult section of the résumé to compose. A well-defined goal captures the attention of decision-makers, and if the goal fits organizational needs, an interview opportunity may follow (Career Planning and Placement Services, 1993). Sport enterprise practitioners prefer to see academic rather than egotistical goals (Cuneen & Sidwell, 1993b). Goal statements that indicate a student's willingness to learn on the job are superior to goals indicating that students are ready to make cutting-edge contributions to their sponsoring organizations (Cuneen & Sidwell, 1993b). For instance, students who have goals of exploring their capabilities in professional settings or refining their entry-level skills are preferable to students whose goals are to share their capabilities with sponsoring organizations or secure a field experience that will lead to permanent employment.

Related Experiences

Students should have an array of academic and sport managerial experiences related to their career objectives (Cuneen & Sidwell, 1993b). Each pre-professional experience and any extracurricular activities should be listed within the student's credential package (Ayers, 1992).

Sponsoring organizations appreciate résumés that identify absolute academic and background qualities more than those that offer general statements of skills (Cuneen & Sidwell, 1993b). For example, frequently selected interns are ones who identify their proficiencies at particular computer hardware and software applications. In contrast, least frequently selected interns present themselves merely as computer literate or experienced in word-processing. Stating that one is proficient on IBM and Macintosh computers and familiar with Lotus 1-2-3, Page Maker, and Cricket Graphics is more effective than stating that one has used spreadsheet applications, desktop publishing and graphics software.

Cover Letters

There are different types of letters that accompany credentials (Career Planning and Placement Services, 1993). Letters of inquiry are used to investigate job availability. Letters of application are used when applying for known job vacancies, and letters of transmittal are used as cover letters to introduce other materials or documents that are being sent under the same cover.

Effective letters motivate employers to examine credentials further. Candidates' letters should be specific; organizations may have several field experience openings in various settings, and it is important that credentials be routed to the proper departments and reviewed by the appropriate decision-makers. Candidates should know the names(s) of persons who will be making decisions in the search/screening process, and letters should be addressed to them. Letters should touch on educational and experiential qualifications but refer readers to the résumé for detailed information. Table 8 provides an appropriate checklist of important components of cover letters (Career Planning and Placement Services, 1993).

Some campus and job placement organizations have all types of sample cover letters on file. They have been prepared after much research into what has been successful and may be an appropriate vehicle for certain enterprises. However, sometimes letters are used by reviewers to evaluate writing and communication skills. Norman (1992) suggests that applicants should not use institutional models but should show their uniqueness by authoring their own. Cost of all materials (paper, envelopes and postage, fax) should be incurred by candidates. Field experience candidates who use institutional or employers' stationery and postal materials may represent themselves as people who are letting others incur expenses for personal searches (Norman, 1992).

When candidates are reasonably certain that credentials have arrived at their destination (about one to three weeks after mailing), they should place phone calls to credentials recipients to verify that the credentials have arrived, and to inquire about any additional questions, dates of possible interviews, date of final decision, and so forth.

Recommendations

Letters of recommendation are testimonials to candidates' academic and work performances. Letters should be solicited from persons who can address the intricacies of field experiences for which candidates are applying and can give specific information concerning candidates' skills, work habits, and abilities (Career Planning and Placement Services, 1993).

The most appropriate persons to write letters of recommendation are former or current employers, supervisors from volunteer experiences, institutional faculty, and others who can attest to candidates' academic and professional competencies. Many times, writ-

Table 8. Important Components of Cover Letters

• Letter is addressed to particular person	• Appreciation is expressed
• Letter contains non-sexist citation (i. e., no "Dear Sir," "Gentleman" or "Madam")	• Letter is original rather than mass produced
• Salutation is followed by colon not comma	• Letter is neat and attractive
• Letter states what positions is being applied for and how writer knew about position	• Spelling, grammar, syntax, punctuation are correct
• Letter states why candidate is interested in the position	• Letter fits on one page
• Letter relays what candidate can do for the organization	• Letter is free of trendy or "canned" phrases
• Specific examples of skills are stated	• Letter is confident but not arrogant
• Letter does not repeat information available in résumé	• Letter is signed in black or blue ink
• Sentence structure is varied and use of words "I" And "my" are limited at the beginning of sentences	• Letter is printed on high-quality paper and matches résumé
• Follow-up phone call is mentioned	• Letter is personal not general

Note: The information in this table is from *Career Search*, (page 45) by Career Planning and Placement Services, 1993. Bowling Green, OH: Bowling Green State University. Copyright © 1993 by Bowling Green State University. Adapted by permission.

ers inquire about the types of information that students would like addressed in the letters. General elements contained in recommendation letters are:

1. A statement of the nature of relationship between the writer and candidate (professional capacity and duration of capacity).
2. A description of the candidates' academic and career growth and potential.
3. A review of important achievements.
4. A review of personal dimensions (what kind of colleague the candidate will make).
5. A summary of candidates' outstanding strengths and abilities.

It takes much time and effort to compose suitable letters of recommendation, so writers need ample time (up to a month) to complete them. Note that when people write letters of recommendation, they are doing a favor for the field experience candidate. They are not required to write, nor are they remunerated for writing; they receive no benefits from writing, other than the satisfaction of helping someone reach a goal (Career Planning and Placement Services, 1993). Field experience candidates should not take advantage of writers' generosity by rushing them, asking them to write several letters, and so forth. Students should provide writers with a current résumé and stamped, pre-addressed (typed) envelopes.

Supporting Documents

Some organizations require documentation to verify résumé listings. Transcripts, writing examples, or graphic products may need to be included in credentials packages. If students are applying for field experiences in sports journalism, reporting, or marketing, examples of professional writing, graphics, or audio/video tapes of students' work may have to accompany credentials. If students have been involved in any research or service projects that resulted in published or unpublished reports or articles, they may also be included.

Unique Credential Requests

In addition to paper credentials, sponsoring organizations can request that field experience candidates submit a videotaped presentation. Contents of the tape may be candidates' responses to a series of questions, an oral presentation of a philosophical position, or an oral summary of pertinent information. Candidates are not obligated to participate in this process, and the organization cannot demand it. However, it is a sound idea to comply. Students applying for certain field experiences such as sports reporting or production may wish to submit any video-taped presentations themselves even if organizations do not request it initially. Examples of on-air quality work can place candidates in better standing to compete with other students.

If field experience candidates submit video tapes, the "program" should be prepared professionally. Local network affiliates and independent broadcasting stations usually will not produce private tapes, but production can be arranged through campus TV stations, college/university instructional media services, and private production houses. Costs for technical assistance, materials, postproduction, facility usage, and other miscellaneous fees will usually be incurred by candidates rather than the organizations that made the requests.

Sponsoring organizations may ask candidates to prepare an audio tape in addition to or in place of video, and some field experience candidates even send audio tapes in place of cover letters or résumés (Sidwell, 1992). Audio production steps are similar to video-tape procedures, but the cost is usually much less.

Credentials Evaluation

Evaluation of paper credentials is a subjective process; decision-makers choose candidates based not only on candidate qualifications but also on their perceptions of how well candidates may fit into their organizations philosophically and socially. Certain biases held by decision-makers may influence personnel decisions (Cuneen & Sidwell, 1993a). Powell (1987) and Hultz, Gardner, and Kozlowski (1988) found that quality of academic performance and major grade point average override any social biases in candidate selection. The similarity of candidates to decision-makers also affects hiring decisions (Graves & Powell, 1988) as do decision-makers' sex-role attitudes (King & King, 1983).

There is less bias in initial personnel screening when abundant, job-relevant information about candidates is available (Gordon & Owens, 1988; Heilman, 1984; Tosi & Einbender, 1985) and when applicants' credentials are congruent with job demands (Plake et al., 1987; Sharp & Post, 1980). These phenomena place limitless importance on credentials preparation, and students should devote as much time to credentials preparation as to the initial screening of appropriate field sites.

Dynamics of Applicant Interviews

Many sport enterprises require interviews of field experience candidates. Visitations are arranged by and at the convenience of the sponsoring organizations. Some organizations with larger field experience programs will fund and arrange candidate travel, but field experience candidates usually make travel and lodging accommodations and absorb all interview costs themselves.

Typically, interviews focus on an overview of the position, a question and answer session, open discussion of the candidate's intentions, and a discussion of the candidate's future plans (Ayers, 1992). Students should be prepared to answer questions about their education, grades, jobs, extracurricular activities, goals, strengths, and weaknesses. Candidates may also be asked to participate in role-playing exercises such as communicating with a difficult client.

Students should acquire all available materials on interview preparation from their institutional career planning and placement offices, and even should request to meet with a counselor trained to prepare students for interviews. Most college/university placement offices give several interview skills workshops per year. Students need to make the time to attend one or more of these sessions.

Candidates may wish to participate in "mock interviews" with colleagues or faculty before participating in actual field experience interviewing processes. *The Northwestern Lindquist-Endicott Report* (1991) contains an extensive list of questions asked frequently by both interviewers and candidates. The report will help candidates clarify their own questions, as well as provide insight into the types of questions they may be asked in interviews. Table 9 lists some common questions asked by employers.

Field experience candidates should request that interviews take place at a time when they can meet and speak with all organization personnel with whom they will be working. Candidates should be prepared and know specific information about the company either through the company's annual report or other materials. In short, candidates should make the decision easy for the agency. They should inquire about types and duration of any field student training sessions. It is important that candidates ask about any future steps in the

Table 9. Summary Of Questions
Employers Ask In Interviews

• What goals have you set?	• How have you changed personally since you entered college?
• What did you consider when choosing your major?	• How do you motivate people?
• What two or three things are most important to you in choosing a position?	• Tell me about a situation when you had to persuade another person to your point of view.
• Tell me about a project you initiated.	• How do you solve conflicts?
• What are your strengths? Weaknesses? How do you evaluate yourself?	• Give an example of a problem you solved and the process used.
• Describe a situation where you had a conflict with another individual and how you dealt with it.	• Describe the project that best demonstrated your analytical skills.

Note: The information in this table is from *The Northwestern Lindquist-Endicott Report* by Victor Lindquist, 1991. Evanston, IL: Northwestern University. Copyright © 1991 by The Placement Center, Northwestern University. Adapted by permission.

interview process. Many organizations require a second interview, even for field experiences. Candidates should also ask "who calls whom" after the interview and inquire about when the hiring decision will be made.

Candidates must, of course, be dressed professionally to make a nonverbal statement about themselves, their programs, and institutions. Candidates presume that they should be attired in "dress-type" outfits or other acceptable business-wear; candidates do not ask interviewers if they should wear suits, skirts, ties, and so forth to the interview. Most career placement officers recommend that interviewees wear conservative clothing of the best quality they can afford (Career Planning and Placement Services, 1993). Candidates might also discern the appropriate attire for specific work environments and dress appropriately.

Unique Interviews

For cost effectiveness, some sponsoring organizations interview via telephone exclusively or at least use phone interviews for initial candidate screening. These communications costs are usually absorbed by the organization. Phone interviews should be arranged when both the candidate and organization representative will be uninterrupted. Candidates should arrange to be interviewed in privacy, perhaps from their faculty advisor's office or from home during times when they will have unobstructed access to their phone and materials.

Many times, especially at larger organizations, personnel decisions are made by field experience panels. Students should be aware that they might be interviewed by more than one person, perhaps even a board or committee (Norman, 1992). It is important to remember names and titles of all interviewers. It is not always clear who from the panel will give final approval.

Again, campus career development and placement offices are the most appropriate resources for interview information. Field experience candidates should take advantage of any student support services available to them on campuses, even if nominal fees are charged.

Actions After the Interview

Candidates must let the organization know that they are still interested in competing for field experiences by sending follow-up letters after interviews. Letters are usually sent no later than two days after candidates return home. Letters should express candidates' appreciation for the interview and mention some key points from the meeting (Career Planning and Placement Services, 1993). If candidates still have not heard from the organization after 10 days to 2 weeks, it is proper to inquire about the status of their credentials.

Candidates also have obligations to inform organizations if they are no longer interested in completing a field experience with them. If candidates accept another opportunity or decide that an organization is not appropriate for their education or career needs, they must inform the organization immediately so the organization can search and screen for another candidate.

Candidates' Rights in Credentials Evaluation and Interview Processes

Candidates are protected from discrimination and other social barriers associated with interviewing and hiring. Interviewers may not seek information that is unrelated to job competency. Students should obtain a list of laws from career placement and planning offices and from any offices for social justice on campus. It is important to remember that laws vary; therefore, candidates should be familiar with any laws inherent to certain states, provinces, and local jurisdictions in which their sponsoring organizations are located. Generally, most states and jurisdictions have laws in place to protect candidates for employment from the following:

Sexual Harassment - Interviewers may not create a hostile environment for candidates through jokes, innuendo, propositions, and so forth. This dimension of law is subject to broad or narrow interpretation depending on circumstances, and enforcement strategies vary.

Personal Habits - Interviewers are limited in the types of questions and information they can gather concerning candidates' personal habits and backgrounds. Health habits, religion, sexual orientation, and so forth may not be discussed. In some counties, states, and provinces, refusals to issue employment contracts for any of these reasons violate the law, and candidates who have been affected have legal recourse.

Requests for Photograph - Just as in video-tape requests, organizations may request photographs, but candidates are not obligated to comply. Photos may be submitted with or without request, but candidates cannot be required to submit photographs of themselves.

Birthdates - Candidates are not obligated to provide birthdates during credential submission or interview. They may volunteer this information during credential screening. If candidates are hired, especially for paid field experiences, birthdates must be furnished for personnel records.

Marital Status - It is illegal for an interviewer to inquire about candidates' present marital status or future plans toward marriage. This information may be volunteered by the candidate.

Family Obligations/Child Care Plans- Employers may not ask questions that are unrelated to the work environment or candidates' qualifications. Questions relating to any family commitments are illegal.

Field experience candidates are generally entitled to the same state and provincial legal protections as those who apply for regular employment. Candidates should be responsible in knowing employment laws that affect them. If students have complaints regarding any interview procedure, they should report it immediately to their major advisors or the sport management field experience coordinator.

On the Job Considerations

Most professions have codes of conduct to which organizations and/or individuals subscribe. The codes are usually related to a professional association and define the mission of the profession and the comportment of those who pursue careers in it. Students should become familiar with any professional associations related to their chosen careers and organizations. They might even consider joining the association; many associations offer reduced membership dues for student members.

Some organizations have policies protecting workers from abusive situations. Students need to be as aware of these as regularly employed workers are aware of them. Most organizations will furnish field students with copies of organizational policies and procedures when students begin their experiences. If the organization does not offer such information, students should ask for copies of any appropriate materials.

Students should also investigate needs for insurance (liability, travel, workers' compensation). Claims may arise out of real or alleged medical incidents or acts of omission. Holders of some types of insurance are protected fully from claims, and many organizations require field students to arrange for insurance. Some institutions require field students to secure blanket liability against claim, and premiums are billed through campus business offices. Field students may also wish to arrange for supplementary travel risk insurance for the length of the field experience if they will be traveling on behalf of the organization, such as for sales, distribution, or meetings.

Financial bonding is imperative if field students are going to be responsible for money or cash reserves in sales, ticket offices, or similar venues. With bonding, an insurance agent issues a policy that guarantees payment of a specified sum to the sponsoring organization in case of financial loss caused by the act of the field student or by some situation over which the field student has no control.

Summary

1. Sponsoring organizations' first clues relative to field experience student suitability are through students' credentials.
2. Credentials must be prepared in a format that best highlights field experience students' experiences and accomplishments.
3. The field experience goal must reflect students' willingness to learn while contributing to sponsoring organizations.
4. Interviews should be rehearsed and critiqued.
5. Students are protected by law from personal, non-work related interview questions and should know the laws of the state or province in which they will be interviewing.

Suggested Readings and Audio Recordings

Ayers, G. (1992, April). *How to secure an internship in athletic training, fitness, leadership or sport management: Practicing professionals tell it like it is* (Cassette Recording No. 204). Reston, VA: American Alliance for Health, Physical Education, Recreation and Dance.

Norman, D. (1992, April). *How to secure an internship in athletic training, fitness, leadership or sport management: Practicing professionals tell it like it is* (Cassette Recording No. 204). Reston, VA: American Alliance for Health, Physical Education, Recreation and Dance.

Northwestern Lindquist-Endicott report. (1991). Evanston, IL: Northwestern University Placement Center.

Suggested Activities

1. Compile a list of practical, volunteer, service, and part-time employment activities. Which résumé format will best highlight employable qualities? Which format best presents qualifications to the potential field sites? Do any potential sponsoring organizations subscribe to a standardized résumé format? If so, how can qualities be highlighted in the format?
2. Formulate one or more field experience goal(s). Do the goals reflect educational aspects of field experiences? Is the goal a good strategic fit with potential sponsoring organizations?
3. Obtain and examine a copy of the *Northwestern Lindquist-Endicott Report* and find the 50 questions that interviewers ask most frequently. Think of suitable responses that might be given to each of the 50 questions posed. Ask the sport management faculty to examine written responses for reasoning. Practice responding to the questions to someone who can critique your oral responses.

4. Refer to the *Northwestern Lindquist-Endicott Report* and find the 25 most frequent questions asked by students during interviews. Determine which of the questions would be suitable to ask during field supervision interviews. Based on the questions in the report, formulate several original questions that relate specifically to potential sponsoring organizations.

5. Arrange for a "mock" interview. Ask the career planning and placement office to contrive an interview session, or ask if there any interview preparation sessions planned. (If any of potential sponsoring organizations conduct panel interviews, ask the career planning office if it would be possible to be interviewed by a group of career officers.)

6. Volunteer to be an interviewer for colleagues. Ask them the same types of questions that might be expected in an actual interview (based upon your research). Analyze their answers. Determine how the questions could have been answered differently or how the candidate's reactions could have been better.

7. Obtain copies of interview guidelines or actual employment laws from those states and provinces where potential interview sites are located. What laws protect candidates? How are candidates protected from interviewers who make inappropriate comments or ask personal questions that are unrelated to work performance? What is the legal recourse if any of the laws are violated?

8. Develop and refine a personal philosophy of sport management. Formulate a definition of sport and how it is possible to have a personal impact on sport management? If candidates are asked to articulate a personal philosophy and communicate aspirations during interviews, it has to be done adeptly.

PART IV

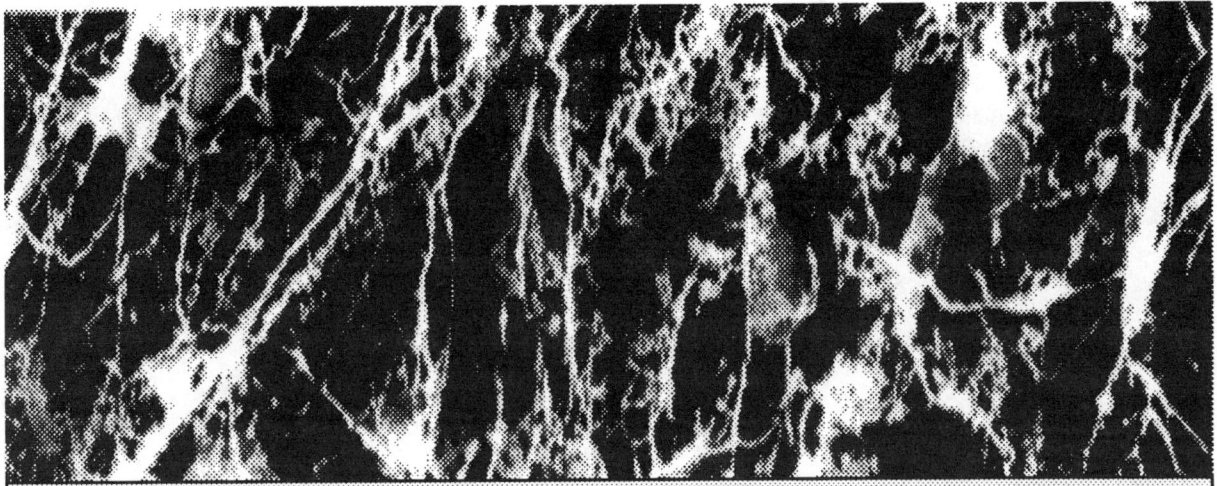

COMPLETING SPORT MANAGEMENT FIELD EXPERIENCES

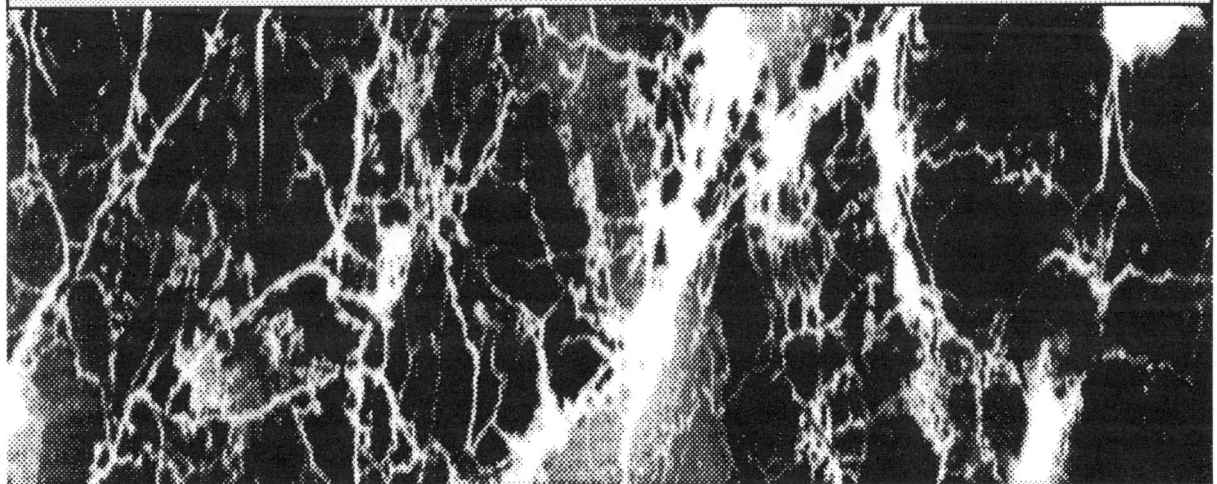

COMPLETING SPORT MANAGEMENT FIELD EXPERIENCES

When students register for field experiences, they reserve spaces for themselves in classes just as if they were going to attend class sessions on campus. Students should expect that their field experiences will be directed by qualified faculty and organizational personnel who function in the best interests of the field students.

Educational Objectives of Field Experiences

Formal evaluation of field students is a collaborative effort between the site supervisor at the sponsoring organization and the university supervisor. Site supervisors provide evaluations as required by the program (midterm, final, etc.), and university supervisors consider those assessments, evaluate required materials submitted by students, and examine other aspects of student performance before assigning final grades (Sidwell, 1984).

Field experiences are subject to the direct supervision of sport management program faculty. As in any academic course, students need to be aware of those educational objectives and/or outcomes associated with their courses of study. Some sport management programs provide course syllabi that outline objectives, requirements, and timelines to field experience students. An example of such a syllabus appears in Appendix A.

The overriding objectives of field experiences are professional maturation and self-evaluation skills (Sidwell, 1984, 1992), and through field experiences, students will be able to:

1. Formulate an awareness of professional responsibilities associated with various areas of sport management
2. Assess the internal dynamics of sport enterprise and industry.
3. Secure practical experiences in specific concentration areas.
4. Formulate professional behavior appropriate to the profession.
5. Formulate interpersonal and professional communication skills.
6. Develop abilities to work and cooperate with colleagues in individual and/or group activities
7. Formulate or enhance a professional network.
8. Evaluate, analyze, and improve time management skills.
9. Evaluate, analyze, and improve stress management skills.
10. Evaluate sport management as a career choice.

During field experiences, sponsoring organizations may request students to perform any number of duties to enlighten them regarding various aspects of sport or event administration. All assignments should relate directly to the educational aspects of field experiences. When both students and sponsoring organizations understand the purposes of field experiences, experiential education can provide a combination of work experiences and learning opportunities linking theory to practice.

Sponsoring organizations have made commitments to both students and sport management programs, and they should have objectives and goals in place (Santesanio, 1992). Field sites should accommodate the following objectives for student learning:

1. Provide opportunities for students to evaluate themselves relative to the field experience and their preparation.
2. Provide opportunities for the faculty and site supervisors to evaluate field students in terms of skills, competencies, and performance.
3. Provide opportunities for students to establish realistic goals for professional development.
4. Provide opportunities to compare and utilize theories and concepts learned in the classroom and related experiences.

Responsibilities and Expectations of Field Students

Stanton and Ali (1987) raised three important points for students regarding field experiences: (a) Students must be active in the learning process, expending energy and taking initiative to ask questions and take on varied, challenging work assignments; (b) students determine what they want to learn and should tap learning resources such as supervisors, faculty, co-workers, and other interns; and (c) students need to monitor their progress continually toward achievement of their learning and goals. The commitments of field students relate to attitude, dependability, communication, and responsibility (Torres, 1987).

Field experience students are considered regular employees in work responsibilities and are integral parts of the sponsoring organizations. They must perform as expected by their site supervisors and maintain a mature, professional demeanor. Students should complete the required number of hours as outlined in sport management program guidelines. Hours recorded at sponsoring organizations should reconcile with the required minimum academic and clock hours. Additional or "overtime" hours are worked at the discretion of the field student.

Students should meet any programmatic requirements such as maintaining any required grade point averages. Field experience procedures for most sport management programs require field students to submit required course materials, present evidence of professional activities, and participate in academic exercises under the direction of their university supervisor(s). Examples of some student learning activities are (Sidwell, 1992):

1. Maintenance of weekly work schedule(s) constituting evidence that field students are meeting the minimum number of clock hours at their field site, and therefore can be awarded full academic hours credit upon field experience completion. An example of a weekly work schedule appears in Appendix B
2. Maintenance of weekly logs showing actual activities performed during work hours, difficult tasks, successful tasks, and self-evaluation of performance for the week. Logs are usually maintained throughout the work week, then delivered to the sport management faculty supervisor by a specified deadline during the following week. An example of a weekly log appears in Appendix B.
3. Cooperation with faculty supervisor(s) attempting to maintain contact. Field students should halt sponsoring organization duties to speak to their supervisor or explain that calls will be returned upon completion of duties. Students might also

be expected to arrange for their site supervisors to be available during a specified time to accommodate conference calls between themselves and the faculty supervisor. Fax and e-mail are also appropriate media for maintaining contact if they are available at both the field site and the institution.

4. Arrangements for observation by a supervising sport management faculty member at their field site. Field students should provide to their supervisor a map with detailed instructions and directional orientation guiding the supervisor to the field experience site. In cases where a critical driving radius has been defined, field students should demonstrate cooperation with faculty via telephone, FAX, e-mail, and so forth.

5. Provision to site supervisors of all required materials related to field experiences and evaluation of field students. These may include forms for midterm and final evaluations, policies and procedures for field experiences, examples of weekly logs and schedule forms, lists of field students requirements, forms for assigning final grades for experiences, and directions for the conduct of an exit interview upon field experience completion.

6. Submission of projects and/or portfolios as required by the sport management program. Some programs, especially for the internship, require students to complete major projects. Examples of these types of projects are (a) a compilation of demographic data relating to typical suiteholders for a professional hockey team's arena; (b) an overview or description of the sponsoring organization itself, with detailed instructions to be used by future field students; (c) a cost analysis of printing and advertising costs for ticket offices, and (d) an analysis of usage patterns by age/gender for a fitness complex. In-depth projects such as these usually are more inherent in internships than practica. For practica, a written, final analysis of the field experience or similar assignment may be the only requirement.

7. Willingness to and availability to communicate regularly with site supervisors. Some organizations require that field students meet weekly with the site supervisor for the purpose of evaluation.

8. Attendance at on-campus seminars, if within reasonable driving radius of an institution's main campus. At these sessions, field students share experiences and concerns related to adjustment, work schedules, educational opportunities, and so forth. This also gives students a structured forum in which to voice their opinions related to the profession.

9. Visit to organizations similar to their sponsoring organization for the purpose of observation and comparison or contrast. Reports of the observations are then submitted either upon completion of the visits or as part of a final field experience portfolio.

10. Complete evaluation instruments (self, site, sponsoring organization supervisor, type of experience, etc.). The self-evaluation is usually confidential, examined only by students' faculty supervisors and/or site supervisors, but evaluations of the sponsoring organization, sponsoring organization supervisor, and experience type may be filed for use by future field students in researching potential field experience sites. Examples of evaluation instruments students may use are available in Appendix C (evaluation of experience), Appendix D (evaluation of sponsoring organization), and Appendix E (evaluation of site supervisor).

11. Participation in an exit interview for the purposes of assessing students' strengths, weaknesses, competencies, professionalism, and so forth. Meetings of this type may be required by the sport management program and/or agencies with more structured field experience programs.

12. Provision of any other periodic self-assessments as required by the sport management program or requested by the faculty supervisor. Field students should be provided with specific criteria upon which to evaluate themselves in terms of improvements, time management, contribution, and other aspects of education served by field experiences.

Responsibilities of the Sport Management Program Field Experience Coordinator

Many sport management programs have designated a faculty member who is committed to the goals and values of experiential education to serve as a field experience coordinator/director. The coordinator is available to assist in the field student's searches and articulate program goals and values to the students, the academic community, and various sponsoring organizations. Some of the functions a coordinator might be expected to perform on behalf of students and sport management programs include:

1. Development of new field experience sites.
2. Evaluation of existing field experience sites.
3. Development and maintenance of a vehicle for disseminating information on appropriate sites to eligible students.
4. Confirmation of student eligibility.
5. Assistance to academic advisors and students searching for appropriate sites.
6. Development and dissemination of forms necessary to complete the field experience registration process.
7. Development of the learning experiences, requirements, and materials to be used by students during their field experience courses.
8. Facilitation of requests for interviews/presentations by organizations seeking field experience students from the program.
9. Establishment and dissemination of all pertinent program and university deadlines to faculty and students.
10. Possession of learning agreements (or contracts) and facilitation of their handling by the university.
11. Assignment of field students to faculty supervisors.
12. Preparation of supervision guidelines for faculty.
13. Development of instruments to be used by site supervisors in evaluating students.
14. Development of instruments used by students to evaluate the sponsoring organization as a site and the sponsoring organization supervisor as mentor.
15. Development of criteria for a capstone, culminating or exit interview experience between students and sponsoring organization supervisors.
16. Sponsorship of orientation sessions for new faculty supervisors.
17. Notification to field students concerning their assigned faculty supervisor and appropriate information for contacting the faculty member.

18. Facilitation for the recording of grades.
19. Dissemination of confirmation letters and expressions of appreciation to sponsoring organizations.
20. Development and maintenance of information files used by students in their search for an appropriate setting.
21. Completion of procedures necessary for students to be covered by university approved insurance programs.
22. Maintenance of communication with sport management faculty and faculty supervisors.
23. Dissemination of a tangible form (e.g., certificate, paperweight or pen with university logo) of appreciation to sponsoring organization personnel who have provided exceptional supervision of an intern.
24. Communication of policies, procedures, and practices to the necessary constituencies.
25. Acceptance and processing of inquiries from agencies desiring to sponsor an experiential learning experience.
26. Communication of inappropriate agencies and/or agencies that have not provided a quality experience.

Responsibilities and Expectations of University/Program/Faculty Supervisors

Parkhouse (1987) found that over 80% of current sport management programs do not provide for on-site visits by faculty. Faculty supervisors safeguard students and the institution while representing field experiences as academic courses that require a campus representative trained to observe educational processes. Faculty supervisors serve as institutional ambassadors who establish mutually beneficial relationships between campuses, businesses, and industrial communities. When circumstances cause students to select sites far from campus, contact between the field student and major program faculty may be problematic, and faculty from sport management programs located nearer the site are sometimes enlisted to supervise.

Supervisors should be available to assist with projects assigned to students by the organization. For example, if a field student working for a small-market broadcast organization is asked to ascertain marketing information relative to viewers of secondary school girls' and boys' tape-delayed basketball contests, the student may need a faculty consultant to help in designing the market study, analyzing data and presenting results.

Faculty supervisors should be available to visit or call the field site, and consult with the site supervisor using the appropriate language inherent to the field. Faculty familiar with currently useful knowledge in particular fields are better able to judge the quality of tasks and assignments completed by field students. They will also be aware of typical complications and accomplishments associated with student field work in a particular area. Faculty should maintain regular contact with field students and site supervisors. They provide materials on supervision, experiential education, and specific objectives of sport management field experiences and assist in interpreting performance standards expectations for both site supervisors and students.

Faculty supervisors are assigned in various ways but are usually full-time faculty or qualified part-time faculty. It benefits students if the faculty supervisor has a background of both theoretical and practical competencies in the specific fields of study for which they have been assigned as supervisors. When students seek assistance in projects or professionally related problems, supervisors who are proficient in specific areas are often able to offer better assistance to students. Although not always possible, supervisors should have previous field supervision experience. Students should expect faculty supervisors to perform the following functions (Sidwell, 1992):

1. During the first few days of the semester or quarter, supervisors should contact the students assigned to them by telephone. Supervisors should provide to field students their office telephone, and fax numbers (home telephone optional at the sole discretion of the supervisor), regular office hours, dates that they may be unavailable due to off-campus commitments such as conferences or other field visits, speculative dates and/or times for their personal field visitations, and tentative dates and/or times for campus seminars. Supervisors should also provide to field students all of this information in writing.

2. Supervisors should maintain constant contact with field experience students. Telephone calls should be placed by supervisors to students every 7 to 10 days for the purpose of checking their progress and making regular evaluations concerning the quality of experiences and performance. Careful notes that chart the progress of the student should be recorded and filed.

3. Supervisors should send formal letters of introduction to designated site supervisor(s), and maintain contact throughout the semester or quarter. Consultations via telephone three to five times per semester or quarter are usual. Agencies appreciate the interest shown by faculty in both the students and their contributions.

4. Supervisors should conduct seminars, preferably one near the beginning and one near the end of the semester or quarter. Field students who are assigned to sites within a specified critical radius of an institution's main campus should be required to participate.

5. Supervisors should visit students located within a specific proximity to the main campus. Visitation calls should be arranged when time is available to consult with field students, observe them in any appropriate tasks, and at a time when the both the faculty and site supervisors can consult privately on the progress of the field students. Generally, the majority of site visitation time is spent with field students. Their consultation time with site supervisors is shorter in duration (usually 15 to 20 minutes).

6. Supervisors are responsible for the evaluation of weekly logs, schedules, and other materials submitted by field students. As in any academic course, concerns relating to progress, quality of experience, and other developmental aspects of learning should be addressed by supervisors.

7. Supervisors are responsible for evaluating final materials such as projects and portfolios and for providing written assessments to students. Of course, final grades for field experience students are assigned by faculty supervisors. Final grades are usually determined by the faculty supervisor through consultation with the sponsoring organization supervisor, and the field student. The final grade should reflect a mix of subjective and objective evaluations of students learning.

Responsibilities and Expectations of Sponsoring Organization/Site Supervisors

Site or field supervisors should know the educational purposes of field experiences. Although site supervisors are not generally educators, they should be willing to contribute to the total education of field students. Site supervisors should be responsible in reading materials provided to them by students and faculty supervisors and willing to ask questions toward clarification of any objectives or educational outcomes that they do not understand. The "hottest" marketing executive in modern sports promotions may be lauded nationally as the person most likely to move executive suites and sky boxes for arena events, but that person may not understand the intricacies of field experience education for students. Students have better learning opportunities and chances to complete appropriate field tasks if they are assigned to a good sport enterprise executive who knows how to train pre-entry professionals.

Students may not want to be involved in field experience sites where their site supervisor will be new to the job. Field students need opportunities to receive organizational insights and supervision from someone who knows the organization and related technologies thoroughly. Site supervisors who have at least two to three years of experience can potentially offer more to field students than those who have just started on their career paths. Berger (1991) suggested that a successful supervisor should be a natural teacher who enjoys young professionals and has time and patience to help them grow.

Site supervisors should be willing to take risks as field students begin to assume responsibilities that can affect the corporate "bottom line." They must be willing to contribute the time required to help students develop strategic, interpersonal, and other skills. Site supervisors are expected to provide quality pre-professional work experiences and periodic verbal and written evaluations of student's work. They should also feel comfortable in suggesting improvements in the sport management field experience program and, to an extent, the academic preparation of students (Sidwell, 1992). Other specific responsibilities that students should expect from site supervisors are (Sidwell, 1992):

1. Site supervisors should complete midterm or final evaluations of field students at the appropriate times. Most sport management programs furnish forms to site supervisors who respond to prepared questions addressing various aspects of students' performances, conducts, and contributions. Examples of evaluation instruments that site supervisors may use are available in Appendices F and G. The instrument contained in Appendix G is based on one used in industry; the evaluation categories were modified to reflect important components and competencies for sport management field experiences. Sometimes, programs ask that site supervisors merely address those aspects in letters written to faculty supervisors.
2. Site supervisors should make themselves available for periodic consultations via telephone with faculty supervisors. Field students' progress needs to be monitored, and site supervisor's perceptions of students' contributions are important. In instances where students' performances are substandard or students are not adjusting to the work environment, supervisors should maintain contact with faculty on a more frequent basis.

3. Site supervisors should perceive themselves as associates in the educational process. They should feel comfortable in offering advice and suggestions to both field students and faculty.

Responsibilities and Expectations of Sponsoring Institutions

Students should expect that institutions offering sport management programs will support the allotment of faculty time for adequate supervision. In the absence of supplemental field experience fees, institutions should be willing to assume costs of telephone, travel, and mailings related to field experience supervision. Institutional commitment to sport management field students should be equal to that afforded student teachers and to other field education programs, such as those in technology, business, accounting, law-related majors, and numerous other experiential education programs.

Special Circumstances

Students completing field experiences encounter many situations requiring decision-making or problem-solving skills (Dudley, 1981), but periodically students are confronted with special circumstances in the unfamiliar work environment. Some phenomena occur in organizations that may require the intervention of a "protector." Field experience students have a luxury that is unavailable to regular employees in special circumstances: the faculty supervisor. Faculty supervisors are sometimes more able and suitable than students to resolve precarious situations and will intervene on behalf of students in solving issues. Before intervening, faculty may advise students to report special circumstances through those appropriate chains of command within sponsoring organizations. If students are not satisfied with results, faculty should be asked to report circumstances through the chain of command themselves. If students remain dissatisfied after faculty intervention, faculty-student-university administrator-organizational manager conferences may be necessary. Circumstances requiring faculty intervention could include but may not be limited to:

Ethical concerns: Numerous ethical concerns arise in organizations of all sizes. Field students have been asked periodically to fabricate sales logs, sports performance statistics, and so forth. For example, a field student is working with an account executive who sells ticket coupon books to local businesses. The executive must sell a minimum number of coupon books per day in order to meet a fixed salary draw. The executive has an especially good selling day with receipts exceeding the amount of the draw. The executive lists only partial sales in the daily report; other receipts are "buried" and will be reported officially on a day when they are needed to cover the draw.

Sexual Harassment: Frequently, students are subjected to hostile environments at the work site. For instance, a field student is consistently subjected to unwanted, unwelcome comments from the site supervisor concerning looks, dress, and social life. The comments are affecting the student's work performance and professional demeanor. Sexual harassment policies differ by state and province and by narrow or broad definition of sexual harassment; students must know their rights and protections under the law.

Work overload: Students are sometimes asked to perform above and beyond their scheduled hours at a field site. Students should be willing to work overtime and welcome opportunities to learn beyond their regularly planned schedules, but abusive situations arise when sites request unreasonable amounts of work from students. For instance, a student consistently volunteers to perform many extra functions, some of which cause the student to remain at the site several hours after the regular release time. The site supervisor is pleased with the student's diligence and assigns extra work that causes the student to remain at the site every night and return many week-ends.

Work underload: Students may be in a position of being underworked. Some organizations agree to sponsor field students, then don't know what to do with them when they arrive, especially if the field experience is extensive, such as internships. For example, a student reports to the site daily and is given filing, courier, and inventory tasks that are completed by noon. Afternoons are spent interacting with office staff.

Unprofessional behavior: Students should be aware of the types of behavior that are expected of someone in a certain profession. Some professionals take short cuts to accomplish goals even though these actions may violate certain codes of conduct and standard procedures. It is entirely possible that students may observe behavior unbecoming to the profession and be influenced to emulate it. For example, a site supervisor must submit a report to the corporate headquarters by a certain date. Standard procedure requires that all reports must be approved by the locally assigned executive vice president. The executive vice president is traveling and will not return in time to approve the report, but because the vice president has never requested that the supervisor make changes in any reports, the supervisor sends the report to corporate headquarters without receiving executive approval.

Illegal behavior: Students may observe or be asked to participate in illegal behavior at their field sites. Sometimes, illegalities are camouflaged for field students as standard operating procedure. Most field experiences proceed without major problems, but occasionally supervising faculty must intervene on behalf of students in cases of inappropriate situations. For instance, a field student working in the purchasing department of a major sports arena is ordered by his site supervisor to report that a micro-computer listed on the bill of lading did not arrive, even though the student is aware that the computer is among the unpacked stock waiting to be added to inventory. The supervisor explains that someone needs the computer to perform work-related tasks at home, and it is quite common for employees to take company equipment to their home offices.

Unjust accusations: Field students, especially those who handle money at ticket offices, race tracks, sales offices, and so forth have been accused of stealing or falsifying records. Students have also become embroiled in controversial decisions, office politics, and power plays. For instance, a student's site supervisor is active in a coalition that supports a certain person for promotion. An opposing coalition presumes the student is as involved as the supervisor, and ramifications from the political struggle affect the student as well as the supervisor.

Replacement of site supervisor: Turnover rates at sport organizations are high. Sometimes, site supervisors are promoted, demoted, fired, or otherwise replaced in corporate structures. It is entirely possible that field students may end up working for a supervisor who did not hire them and will not use them properly. For example, a student has been working with the site supervisor as part of a strategic planning team. The supervisor is transferred to another office. The replacement supervisor assigns the student to office support duties such as filing, duplicating, and courier services.

Cessation of field experience: Any large or small enterprise can declare bankruptcy, disband business, move headquarters, or restructure for various reasons. Field students may have their positions terminated unexpectedly. For instance, a field student is an events programmer for a small fitness center. The center merges with another fitness club, and planned programs are not going to be offered anymore. The fitness center informs the student that an events programmer is no longer needed.

Suggested Readings

Dudley, J. S. (Ed.). (1981). *Expand your options*. Washington, DC: National Society for Internships and Experiential Education.

Santesanio, D. (1992). *Sports administration internship guidelines*. Austin, TX: University Internship Services.

Torres, T. (1987). That wonderful resource: The intern. *Employee Services Management, 30*(30), 15-17.

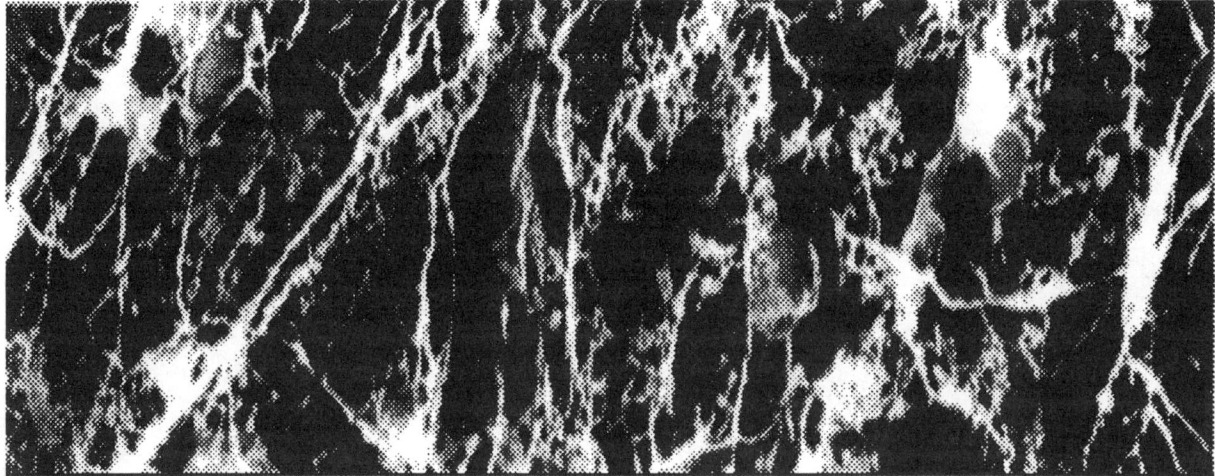

PART V

ACADEMIC EXERCISES
FOR FIELD EXPERIENCE
STUDENTS

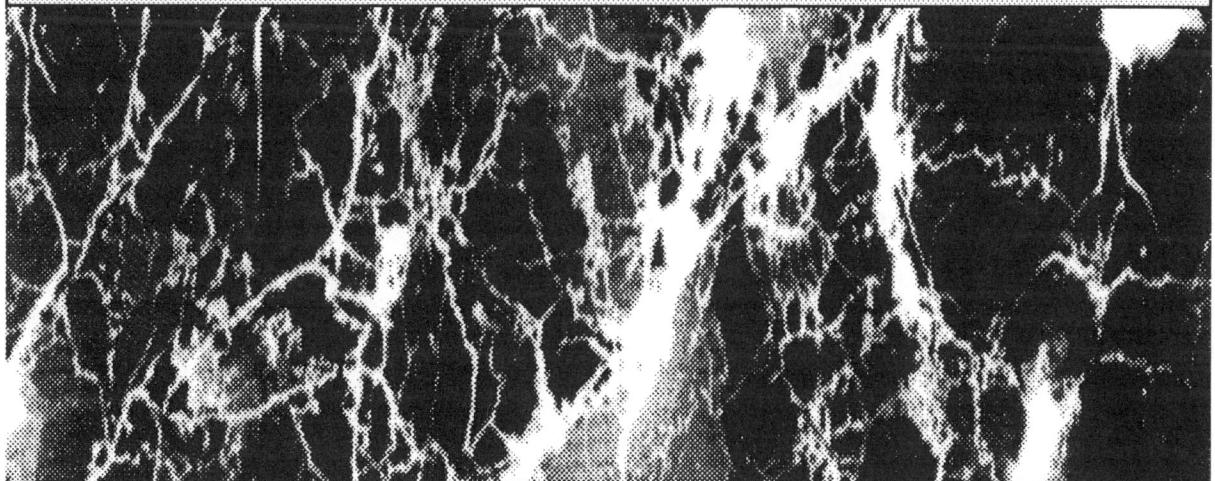

ACADEMIC EXERCISES FOR
FIELD EXPERIENCE STUDENTS

The practical work experiences offered by most agencies are such that students perform similar tasks each day and may not have opportunities to learn about sport organizations in the macro-perspective. Field experiences will be more valuable to students if they are provided opportunities to assess organizational processes and systems rather than just to perform technical tasks. Students may be required to demonstrate that they have learned not just the practical aspects of their assignments, but that they also have a vast overview of how different facets of organizations function individually toward organizational goals or strategies.

Students need to observe how problems, solutions, successes, disagreements, organizational changes, and so forth are influenced by each facet. To demonstrate that students have not only practiced on-the-job skills, but also have observed the sport organization as a whole, students might submit some or all of the following reports to their faculty supervisors:

Continuous Report: Work Log

Daily or weekly logs or reports are used to encourage student reflection about their field experiences. Students may submit a brief description of their work performed each day, describing any new experiences, those experiences for which they felt especially prepared, those for which they felt underprepared, skills that they feel they need to improve, and strategies for improving those skills. A guide for such a log appears in Appendix B.

Report # 1: Organizational Mission

Each organization usually has a mission expressed in writing, a statement that defines organizational purposes and sometimes goals. Each decision and function of the organization should relate directly to this mission. Students may submit an extended report detailing the organization's formal mission and describe those decisions and functions that contributed to the mission during the first week of the field experience. They may also include how field experience students may contribute to organizational mission.

Report # 2: Organizational Chart

Organizational charts describe the management structure and lines of authority within an entire organization. The charts contain names and titles of officials, and some organizations furnish these to new field students and regular employees. In some instances, only job titles are listed, and names of officials are absent, due to managerial turnover and other phenomena unique to the organization itself. Students may develop an organizational chart for their faculty supervisors. Students' charts should reflect both names and titles of all managerial personnel. If students include a line for "Vice Presidents—Finance & Budget," then names of all vice presidents responsible for budgeting and financial aspects of the organization should be listed. Field students who are with smaller organizations, such as local sporting goods retailers or privately owned fitness centers, submit less complicated charts; but even at smaller agencies, there are still lines of management and authority that relate to organizational structure.

Report # 3: Lines of Authority

Understanding the systems of organizational charts is critical. Students should take the chart created in Report #2 and explain how it operates. For instance, in "line authority," power "flows down" because all decisions are made by the person at the "top" of the chart and those "below" merely react to that person's decisions. If decisions are made by the person at the "top" after consultation with and input from those whose names appear "below," then the organization subscribes to "staff authority." If those whose names appear "below" the "top" actually have decision-making authority within their departments, then the organization subscribes to "functional authority." Students may submit an extended explanation of the dimensions of the organization chart.

Report # 4: Strategic Fit of Field Experience Students

Students need to understand the fit of field students in their sponsoring organizations. Students may refer to the organizational charts created in Reports #2 and 3 and show the placement of field students in the structure. They should describe the contribution of field students to organizational effectiveness and comment on how field students contribute to the organization in terms of work assignments and decisionmaking (i.e., are the tasks assigned enabling field students to enhance their managerial skills?). Students may also comment on the organizational alternative to field students (i.e., who would complete their tasks if the sponsoring organization had no field students?).

Report # 5: RACI Charting

Responsibility charting (Galbraith, 1973) clarifies and shapes formal organizational structure by taking various organizational tasks and identifying the roles and relationships of decision-makers and support members. Bolman & Deal (1988) described RACI as the language of this organizational charting process that shows groups on a more intricate level than typical organizational charts. In RACI terms, "R" refers to the person(s) directly RESPONSIBLE for a particular task. "A" refers to the person(s) who must APPROVE a task upon completion but before implementation. "C" refers to the person(s) who must be CONSULTED during the decision-making process. "I" indicates those persons who need to be INFORMED as decisions are made or actions are taken. Table 10 is a RACI chart that may describe the decision-making process in a sport marketing department where the president has decided that advertising expenses have to be cut by 8%.

Table 10. Sample RACI Chart For Marketing Plan

	President	VP-Operations	Marketing Director	Copywriter
Cost Analysis	I	I	R	I
Media Analysis	I	I	R	I
Options Analysis	C	C	R	C
New "Ad" plan	A	A	R	I

Note: The RACI Charting format was adapted from *Modern Approaches to Understanding and Managing Organizations* (page 54) by L. G. Bolman and T. E. Deal, 1988. San Francisco, CA: Jossey-Bass Publishers. Copyright © 1984 by Jossey-Bass Inc., Publishers.

Table 10 indicates that the marketing director is responsible for the cost analysis, media analysis, formulation of alternative plans, and development of the new advertising plan. However, the director must inform or consult with the president, vice-president, and copywriter on various aspects of the decision. Although the director assumes the responsibility at each step, the president and vice-president approve the final decision, in this case, the new advertising plan.

Students may describe a decision that has been made at the sponsoring organization and show the contributions of personnel who were involved in the decision.

Report # 6: Communications Methods and Effectiveness

Communication in any organization, regardless of its size, is a key to effective management. Usually, directives, changes in policy or procedure, daily functions, and so forth are communicated in writing to eliminate the unreliable characteristics of verbal communications. Organizations may have a standard format for communications; formats may be individually related and/or color coded to different departments or lines of authority, or they may be numerically coded for e-mail or fax. Students may describe the communication characteristics of their sponsoring organization. They may comment on the communication effectiveness and process and suggest ways in which communication could be improved. They may also cite examples of effective communication and ineffective communication as observed.

Reports # 7-10: Organizational Frames

Bolman and Deal (1988) described organizations in terms of "frames" that are inherent to all types of functioning business groups:

Structural frame: Emphasizes formal roles and relationships, created to fit an organization's environment and technology. Organizations allocate responsibilities to participants and create rules, policies, and management hierarchies to coordinate diverse activities.

Humanistic frame: Organizations adjust in order to find an organizational form that will enable people to get the job done while feeling good about what they are doing. This frame establishes itself because organizations are inhabited by people with needs, feelings, prejudices, skills, and limitations. People have great capacities to learn and an even greater capacity to defend old attitudes and beliefs. When human needs are ignored, problems arise.

Political frame: Power and influence constantly affect the allocation of scarce resources among individuals or groups. Conflict is expected due to differences in needs, perspectives, and life-styles. Bargaining, coercion, and compromise are evident daily, and coalitions form around specific interests as issues surface. Political skill and acumen lead to solutions.

Symbolic frame: Assumptions of rationality that appear in other frames are abandoned. Organizations are bonded together more by shared values and culture than by goals and policies. They are propelled by rituals, ceremonies, stories, heroes, and myths rather than by rules, policies, and managerial authority. It is problematic when symbols lose meaning, and ceremonies and rituals lose potency.

Table 11 contains examples that might be typical of a sports programming syndication organization. Within large organizations, such as professional sport, collegiate athletics, international or amateur sport governance, and special population sport events, some departments or divisions may function under different frames. Organizations are also capable of changing frames in different circumstances or during different peak work times. Typically, organizations show all aspects of the four frames, but some employees or observers can view the organization and see different frames predominate because of their own sensitivities.

For Reports # 7-10, students may observe the organization and submit reports addressing the four frame perspectives.

Report # 11: Situational Leadership

Managers and/or organizational officials may use different styles of leadership behavior or management. Hersey and Blanchard (1982) described a situational approach to personnel management based on relationships between the amount of direction and control a leader gives (directive behavior), the amount of support and encouragement a leader provides (supportive behavior), and the competence and commitment (developmental level) that a follower exhibits in specific task performance. They suggested four leadership styles:

Directing behavior: High directive/low supportive behavior in which a leader provides specific instructions and supervises task accomplishment closely.

Coaching behavior: High directive/high supportive behavior in which a leader explains decisions yet solicits suggestions and continues to direct accomplishments of tasks.

Supporting behavior: High supportive/low directive behavior in which a leader makes decisions with the follower and supports efforts toward task accomplishment.

Delegating behavior: Low supportive/low directive behavior in which a leader delegates decisions and responsibilities for implementation to followers.

Table 11. Organizational Frames

Sports Programming Syndicator

Structural: Policies and regulations related to acquisition and production of programs exist so the organization is consistent from office to office in several locations. If an office in Tampa operated differently from an office in Portland, then assignment and transfer of staff would be problematic in game and event broadcasts. Tasks are performed uniformly from site to site.

Humanistic: A production crew chief is assigned to work at a college tennis match in Tucson, but her son is playing in a college tennis match in Los Angeles, which is also scheduled to be broadcast. The syndicator reassigns the crew chief to the Los Angeles site.

Political: Some announcers have mobilized in order to discuss the possibilities of collective bargaining for the broadcast talent. A counter-coalition forms supporting individual salary and benefits negotiations.

Symbolic: Each month, if the account executives generate a certain amount of national-level advertising revenue, the management sponsors a lunch for the office staff at a trendy restaurant.

Table 12 gives examples of situational behavior from an arena management group. Students may submit a report that compares and contrasts leader behavior and follower competence and committment at their sponsoring organization.

Report #12: Power and Influence Observation

Power is the ability to order. Influence describes the extent to which one can intervene successfully. For example, a director of marketing can order a copywriter to slant advertising toward certain demographic groups. A market analyst cannot issue those orders, but can convince the director that advertising copy should be targeted for a special group. In this scenario, the director has the power; the analyst has the influence.

Students may submit an extended report showing how power and influence interact at the sponsoring organization. (The intention of this exercise will be solely to generate thought; reports should be shared only with university faculty supervisors.)

Report # 13: Compromise

In every organization, especially larger ones that function through group decisions or the interaction of individual preferences, the ability of people or departments to compromise often contributes to organizational effectiveness. For example, the managers of an organization that owns and operates children's gymnasium franchises have always catered to

Table 12. Leadership Styles

Arena Management Group

Directing: A supervisor of operations assigns the arena crew to set up for a lacrosse game. The supervisor does not consult with anyone on the crew and offers no positive support toward task accomplishment. Subordinates are merely given procedural instructions and are watched closely until the lacrosse set-up is completed.

Coaching: A supervisor of operations assigns the crew to tear down the lacrosse set in order to prepare for a concert tour at the arena. The supervisor offers to be available for questions and comments and gives positive support toward the accomplishment.

Supporting: A supervisor of operations asks the crew about the best ways to use their skills when a tennis match is scheduled for the morning and afternoon and a basketball game is scheduled for the evening. The supervisor accepts the crew's suggestions and helps them accomplish the task.

Delegating: The supervisor of operations authorizes the crew director to decide how to prepare the arena for a circus tour stop. The supervisor does not inquire about the plan or check on the crew's progress.

Note: Developmental Level refers to the responsibility, commitment, and accountability of the subordinate. Some subordinates need little direction and/or support in order to accomplish tasks successfully. Some subordinates require a great deal of direction and support. Leader behavior can vary depending on subordinate behavior.

pre-schoolers. A local franchise operator suggests that equipment and programs should be changed in order to attract children of primary school age. The managers resist the change of mission, but agree to test the market for primary school-aged children by adding appropriate equipment and programs to their existing franchises.

Students may submit an extended report describing a compromise they observed at the sponsoring organization. The report should include an analysis of the compromise process and should address the effectiveness of the compromise. (The intention of this exercise will be solely to generate thought; reports should be shared only with university faculty supervisors.)

Report # 14: Organizational Change

Personnel turnover, shifts in the importance of certain tasks, and personnel reassignment are common to all organizations. Students may describe any managerial changes in the sponsoring organizations. They should describe the circumstances of the change (a new manager is hired due to the release or promotion of the former one, etc.), the atmosphere of the organization as a result of the change, and the behavior of the regular employees as a result of the change.

If there have been no managerial changes, students may describe any changes due to shifts in power or influence or describe changes occurring due to new directions in production, technology and so forth. (The intention of this exercise will be solely to generate thought; reports should be shared only with university faculty supervisors.)

Report # 15: Time and Stress Observation

Many times, organizations do not meet goals, or tasks are not completed due to poor time and stress management skills of those involved in the process. Students may describe how their personal time is managed and how any episodes of stress were resolved during a specific day or week. This report should describe field students' personal experiences, as well as address organizational personnel who were affected by students' experiences. (The intention of this exercise will be solely to generate thought; reports should be shared only with university faculty supervisors.)

Report # 16: Observations of Similar Organization

Students should be familiar with other organizations that operate in ways similar to those of their own field sites. Students may visit one or more organizations that are similar to the one in which they are completing their own field experiences to compare and contrast mission, goals, strategies, facilities and other practical knowledge learned at their own field site with those of similar organizations. Barrett (1983) isolated three basic components of physical skills observation that relate to present purposes: deciding what to observe, planning how to observe, and knowing what factors influence one's ability to observe.

Deciding what to observe: Field students must decide what to look for. They should notice if the chains of command are similar to those of the student's own field organization. Are mission, goals, and strategies to meet mission similar to those at the student's site? Are the functions of workers the same? Are facilities and equipment and/or supplies comparable? If not, why? Which features are unique, and which are similar?

Planning how to observe: Observations of the present kind can be best completed if field students are permitted to interact with agency personnel. Site visitations should be scheduled at a time when field students can interview those personnel whose responsibilities are linked to their own. Students may also wish to ask to see work examples and any policies and procedures guidelines.

Knowing what factors influence one's ability to observe: Observations are influenced by numerous factors:
1. Distraction: Students should conduct their visitations, observations, and interiews in a private place so as to eliminate extraneous factors that may interfere with the conduct of the task.

2. Time allotment: Visitations should be arranged when appropriate agency personnel have more than a few minutes to spend with the field student. In return, field students should have prepared questions/comments arranged logically in order to use time wisely.

3. Schedule of those being observed: Professionals' schedules are subject to unplanned change. In order to interact adequately, field students should request that they be notified of any schedule problems, if possible. The responsibility is with the student to communicate the number of minutes necessary to complete an adequate observation; most professionals will expect that the session will not extend beyond the requested time.

Report # 17: Field Experience Summary

Students may submit a report summarizing their field experience. Reports such as these condense the learning experiences for students and faculty supervisors. The reports can be kept on file to serve as a decision-assistance tool for any future field experience students. Information contained in the summary might include:

Student-related information: Job specifications, description, and duties; living arrangements; compensation.

Overview of the organization: Organizational mission and chart from Mission and Organizational Charts Reports; description of services; description of department (including job descriptions of key personnel, their preparation, and evolution of their careers).

Marketing or public relations: Current materials; the ways in which advertising, promotions, and public relations are used by the agency; appropriate publications.

Finance and budgeting: Description of budget process; description of purchasing process; accounting procedures; annual reports.

Operation and events management: Description of procedures; required personnel and duties.

Program planning: Ways in which activities are selected and prioritized; scheduling; evaluation.

Facilities: Overview and description; diagram and layout; strengths and weaknesses.

Evaluation of placement: Strengths; weaknesses; opinions; recommendations concerning agency; recommendations to future interns.

Exit Interview

Students may desire or be required to participate in an exit interview conducted by the site supervisor. Exit interviews might address students' strengths, weaknesses, and contributions to the organization during their field experiences, career paths advice, advice on job searches, etc. and methods of networking for employment searches.

Final Seminar

Students may be expected to attend a final seminar at which all field students from the current academic term will be present. Some institutions use the seminars to let field students propose changes in field experience policies or suggest improvements in the sport management preparation program. In cases where students cannot return to campus (due to distance, appointments for that day at the site, etc.), conference calls can be arranged.

Major Assignment: Field Experience Project

Students may be required to complete a major project that demonstrates not only the skills they used for the field experience but also their lasting contribution to their sponsoring organization. Projects usually involve continuous attention and should be started early in the field experience. They are monitored closely by both the faculty and site supervisors.

Final Evaluation of Field Experience Student

Final evaluations are usually based on specific programmatic criteria as determined by the sport management faculty. Evaluations may take the form of pass/fail, satisfactory/ unsatisfactory, or letter/numerical grade. Final grade criteria may be based on any proportions of points for combinations of projects, logs, reports/assignments, midsemester and final evaluations by site supervisors, or certain requirements of a student portfolio, such as personal evaluations of the agency/site, evaluation of agency supervisor, results of exit interview, or any other materials deemed appropriate by the sport management faculty.

Suggested Readings

Bolman, L. G., & Deal, T. E. (1988). *Modern approaches to understanding and managing organizations*. San Francisco: Jossey-Bass Publishers.

Galbraith, J. (1973). *Designing complex organizations*. Reading, MA: Addison-Wesley.

Hersey, P., & Blanchard, K. H. (1982). *Management of organizational behavior: Utilizing human resources*. Englewood Cliffs, NJ: Prentice-Hall, Inc.

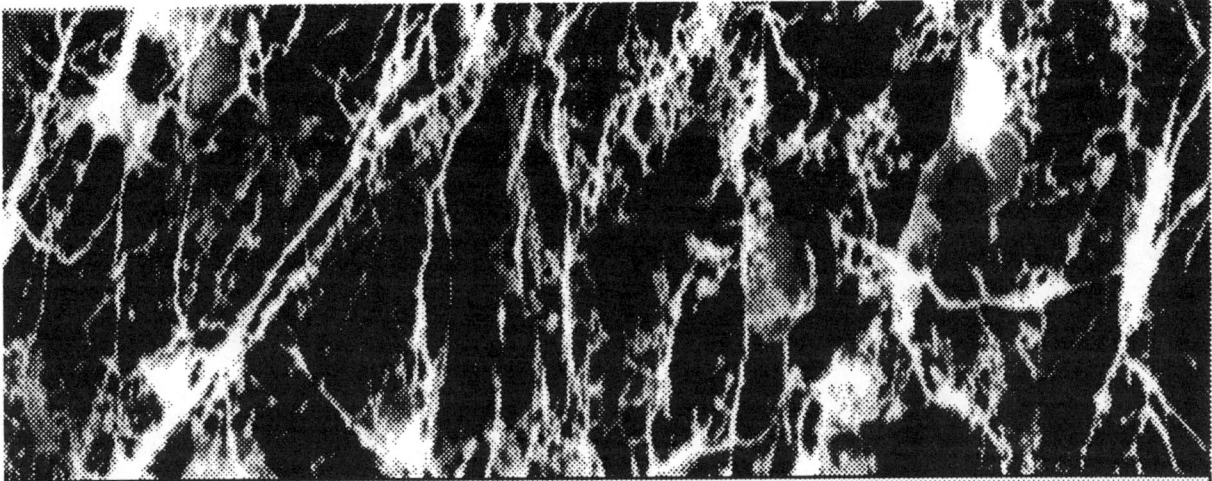

REFERENCES

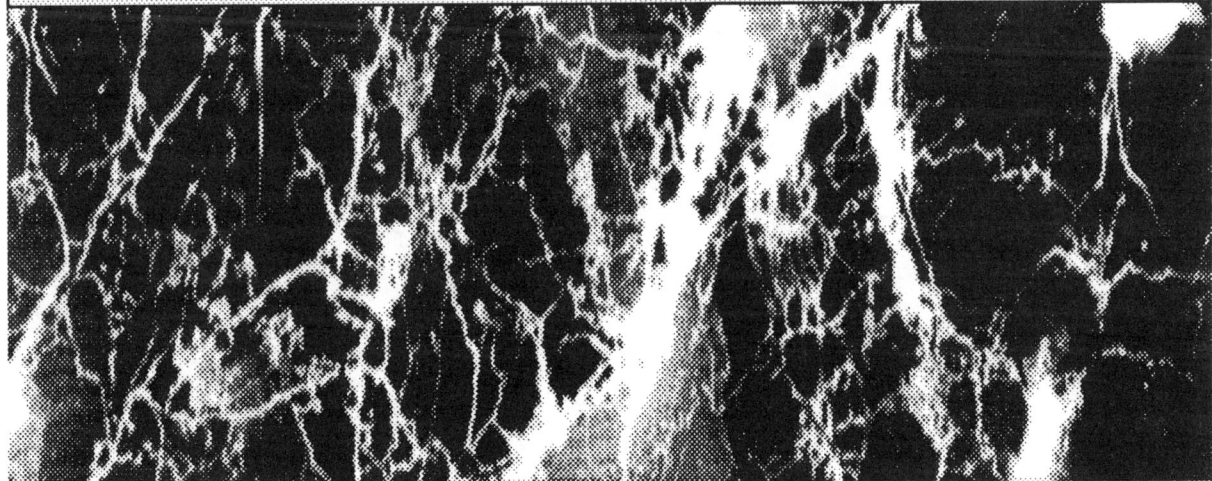

REFERENCES

Ayers, G. (1992, April). *How to secure an internship in athletic training, fitness, leadership or sport management: Practicing professionals tell it like it is* (Cassette Recording No. 204). Reston, VA: American Alliance for Health, Physical Education, Recreation and Dance.

Barrett, K. (1983). A hypothetical model of observing as a teaching skill. *Journal of Teaching in Physical Education, 3*(1), 22-31.

Bauza, W. P. (1984). Values of field experiences. In B. K. Zanger & J. B. Parks (Eds.), *Sport management curricula: The business and education nexus* (pp. 93-94). Bowling Green, OH: Bowling Green State University.

Bell, J. A., & Cousins, J. R. (1993). Professional service through sport management internships. *Journal of Physical Education, Recreation and Dance, 64*(7), 45-52.

Berger, J. (1991). Making an internship work. *Public Relations Journal, 47*(4), 30-31.

Bialac, D., & Wallington, C. (1985). From backpack to briefcase. *Training and Development Journal, 39*(5), 66-68.

Blensley, D. L. (1982). Internships: A personal account. *Journal of Accountancy, 154*, 8-49.

Bolles, R. N. (1987). *The three boxes of life: And how to get out of them.* San Francisco: Ten Speed Press.

Bolman, L. G., & Deal, T. E. (1988). *Modern approaches to understanding and managing organizations.* San Francisco: Jossey-Bass Publishers.

Brassie, P. S. (1989). Guidelines for programs preparing undergraduate and graduate students for careers in sport management. *Journal of Sport Management, 3*(2), 158-164.

Brightman, D. E. (1989). How to build an internship program. *Public Relations Journal, 45*(1), 29-30.

Brown, S. C. (1992, June). *Student preparation for site selection.* Paper presented at the annual meeting of the North American Society for Sport Management, Knoxville, TN.

Career Planning and Placement Services. (1993). *Career Search.* Bowling Green, OH: Bowling Green State University.

Chickering, A. (1976). *Experience and learning: An introduction to experiential learning.* New Rochelle, NY: Change Magazine Press.

Cornell University. (1986). *Learning from field experience: An ethnographic approach to experiential education.* Ithaca, NY: New York State College of Human Ecology.

Ciofalo, A. (1992). What every professor and work-site supervisor should know about internships. In A. Ciofalo (Ed.), *Internships: Perspectives on experiential learning* (pp. 3-7). Malabar, FL: Krieger Publishing Company.

Crookham, J. (1993). Cities bent on sports to boost economy. *Athletic Business, 17*(1), 18-19.

Cuneen, J. (1992). Graduate level professional preparation for athletic directors. *Journal of Sport Management, 6*(1), 15-26.

Cuneen, J., & Sidwell, M. J. (1993a). Effect of applicant gender on rating and selection of undergraduate sport management interns. *Journal of Sport Management, 7*(3), 216-227.

Cuneen, J., & Sidwell, M. J. (1993b). Sport management interns: Selection qualifications. *Journal of Physical Education, Recreation and Dance, 64*(1), 91-95.

Cylkowski, G. (1986). A sporting career. *Business Week Careers, 5*(4), 18-23.

DeSensi, J. T., Kelley, D. R., Blanton, M. D., & Beitel, P. A.. (1990). Sport management curricular evaluation and needs assessment: A multifaceted approach. *Journal of Sport Management, 4* (1), 31-58.

Dudley, J. S. (Ed.). (1981). *Expand your options*. Washington, D C: National Society for Internships and Experiential Education.

Gabris, G. T., & Mitchel, K. (1992). Exploring the relationships between intern job performance, quality of education experience, and career placement. In A. Ciofalo (Ed.), *Internships: Perspectives on Experiential Learning* (pp. 179-194). Malabar, FL: Krieger Publishing Company.

Galbraith, J. (1973). *Designing complex organizations*. Reading, MA: Addison-Wesley.

Gordon, R. A., & Owens, S. D. (1988). The effect of job level and amount of information on the evaluation of male and female job applicants. *Journal of Employment Counseling, 25*(4), 160-161.

Graves, L. M., and Powell, G. N. (1988). An investigation of sex discrimination in recruiters' evaluations of actual applicants. *Journal of Applied Psychology, 73*(1), 20-29.

Gregory, J. (1984). Coordinating the selection and assignment procedure for field experience student. In B. K. Zanger & J. B. Parks (Eds.), *Sport management curricula: The business and education nexus* (pp. 84-85). Bowling Green, OH: Bowling Green State University.

Gryski, G. S., Johnson, G. W., & O'Toole, L. J., Jr. (1992). Undergraduate internships: An empirical review. In A. Ciofalo (Ed.), *Internships: Perspectives on experiential learning* (pp. 179-194). Malabar, FL: Krieger Publishing Company.

Heilman, M. E. (1984). Information as a deterrent against sex discrimination: The effects of applicant sex and information type on preliminary employment decisions. *Organizational behavior and human performance,33*(2), 174-186.

Hersey, P., & Blanchard, K. H. (1982). *Management of organizational behavior: Utilizing human resources*. Englewood Cliffs, NJ: Prentice-Hall, Inc.

Hollingsworth, P. (1990). The case for interns. *Folio, 19*, 131-132.

Hultz, B. M., Gardner, P. D., & Kozlowski, S. W. J. (1988). *Screening job applicants: Recruiter decision strategies*. (Report No. CE 051 398). East Lansing, MI: Michigan State University Collegiate Employment Research Institute. (ERIC Document Reproduction Service No. ED 301 664).

King, D. W., & King, L. A. (1983). Sex-role egalitarianism as a moderator variable in decision-making: Two validity studies. *Educational and Psychological Measurement, 43*((4), 1199-1210.

Mason, J. G., Higgins, C., & Wilkinson, O. (1981). Sports administration education 15 years later. *Athletic Purchasing and Facilities, 5,* 44-45.

McClam, T., & Kessler, M. H. (1982). Human service internships. *Journal of College Placement, 42*(2), 45-47.

Miller, R. (1984). Sport management field experiences with the Detroit tigers baseball club. In B. K. Zanger & J. B. Parks (Eds.), *Sport management curricula: The business and education nexus* (pp. 86-88). Bowling Green, OH: Bowling Green State University.

National Association for Girls and Women in Sport. (1991). *NAGWS guide to internships: Climbing the corporate ladder*. Reston, VA: American Alliance for Health, Physical Education, Recreation and Dance.

National Association for Sport and Physical Education/North American Society for Sport Management. (1993). *Sport management program standards and review protocol*. Reston, VA: Author.

Norman, D. (1992, April). *How to secure an internship in athletic training, fitness, leadership or sport management: Practicing professionals tell it like it is* (Cassette Recording No. 204). Reston, VA: American Alliance for Health, Physical Education, Recreation and Dance.

Northwestern -Lindquist-Endicott report. Evanston, IL: Northwestern University Placement Center.

Parkhouse, B. L. (1984). Shaping up to climb a new corporate ladder ... sport management. *Journal of Physical Education, Recreation and Dance, 55*(7),12-14.

Parkhouse, B. L. (1987). Sport management curricula: Current status and design implications for future development. *Journal of Sport Management, 1*(1), 93-115.

Parks, J. B. (1991). Employment status of alumni of an undergraduate sport management program. *Journal of Sport Management, 5*(2), 100-110.

Parks, J. B., & Olafson, G. A. (1987). Sport management and a new journal. *Journal of Sport Management, 1*(1), 1-3.

Parks, J. B., & Quain, R. J. (1986). Sport management survey: Curriculum perspectives. *Journal of Physical Education, Recreation and Dance, 57*(4), 22-26.

Parks, J. B., & Zanger, B. R. K. (1990). *Sport & fitness management career strategies and professional content*. Champaign, IL: Human Kinetics Books.

Patton, P. L., & Dial, D. F. (1988). Testing the water: A survey on HRD internships. *Training and Development Journal, 42*(10), 48-51.

Plake, B. S., Murphy-Berman, V., Derscheid, L. E., Gerber, R. W., Miller, S. K., & Tomes, R. E. (1987). Access decisions by personnel directors: Subtle forms of sex bias in hiring. *Psychology of Women Quarterly, 11*(2), 255-263.

Powell, G. N. (1987). The effects of sex and gender on recruitment. *Academy of Management Review, 12,* 731-743.

Quain, R. J., & Parks, J. B. (1986). Sport management survey: Employment perspectives. *Journal of Physical Education, Recreation and Dance, 57*(4),18-21.

Ricchiute, D. N. (1980, July). Internships and the local practitioner. *Journal of Accountancy,* 35-46.

Santesanio, D. (1992). *Sports administration internship guidelines*. Austin, TX: University Internship Services.

Schon, D. A. (1983). *The reflective practitioner*. San Francisco: Jossey-Bass.

Schon, D. A. (1987). *Educating the reflective practitioner*. San Francisco: Jossey-Bass.

Sharp, C., & Post, R. (1980). Evaluation of male and female applicants for sex-congruent and sex-incongruent jobs. *Sex Roles, 6,* 391-401.

Sidwell, M. J. (1984). The sport management field experience profile at Bowling Green State University. In B. K. Zanger & J. B. Parks (Eds.), *Sport management curricula: The business and education nexus* (pp. 79-83). Bowling Green, OH: Bowling Green State University.

Sidwell, M. J. (1992). *Student guide for sport management practica*. Bowling Green, OH: Bowling Green State University.

Stanton, T., & Ali, K. (1987). *The experienced hand: A student manual for making the most of an internship*. Cranston, RI: Carroll Press Publishers.

Sutton, W. A. (1989). The role of internships in sport management curricula: A model for development. *Journal of Physical Education, Recreation and Dance, 60*(7), 20-24.

Taylor, M. S. (1984). Strategies and sources in the student job search. *Journal of College Placement, 45*(1), 40-45.

Taylor, M. S. (1988). Effects of college internships on individual participants. *Journal of Applied Psychology, 73*(3), 393-401.

Taylor, M. S., & Dunham, R. B. (1980, October). A program for planned student and personnel practitioner interests. *Personnel Administrator, 25*(10), 35-37.

Torres, T. (1987). That wonderful resource: The intern. *Employee Services Management, 30*(30), 15-17.

Tosi, H. L., & Einbender, S. W. (1985). The effects of the type and amount of information in sex discrimination research: A meta-analysis. *Academy of Management Journal, 28*(3), 712-723.

United States Department of Labor. (1991). *A report on the glass ceiling initiative*. Washington, DC: U. S. Government Printing Office.

Verner, M. E. (1993). Developing professionalism through experiential learning. *Journal of Physical Education, Recreation and Dance, 64*(7), 45-52.

Washburn, J. R. (1984). What does academe need from business/agencies? Supervision: A participatory activity. In B. K. Zanger & J. B. Parks (Eds.), *Sport management curricula: The business and education nexus* (pp. 79-83). Bowling Green, OH: Bowling Green State University.

Wurfel, W. W. (1985). Well-nurtured interns can reap benefits and bring rewards. *Public Relations Journal, 41*(4), 37.

Young, D. (1990a). Implementing the practical experience for the graduate sport management student. *Illinois Journal of Health, Physical Education, Recreation and Dance, 37*, 15-16.

Young, D. (1990b). Mentoring and networking: Perceptions by athletic administrators. *Journal of Sport Management, 4*, 71-79.

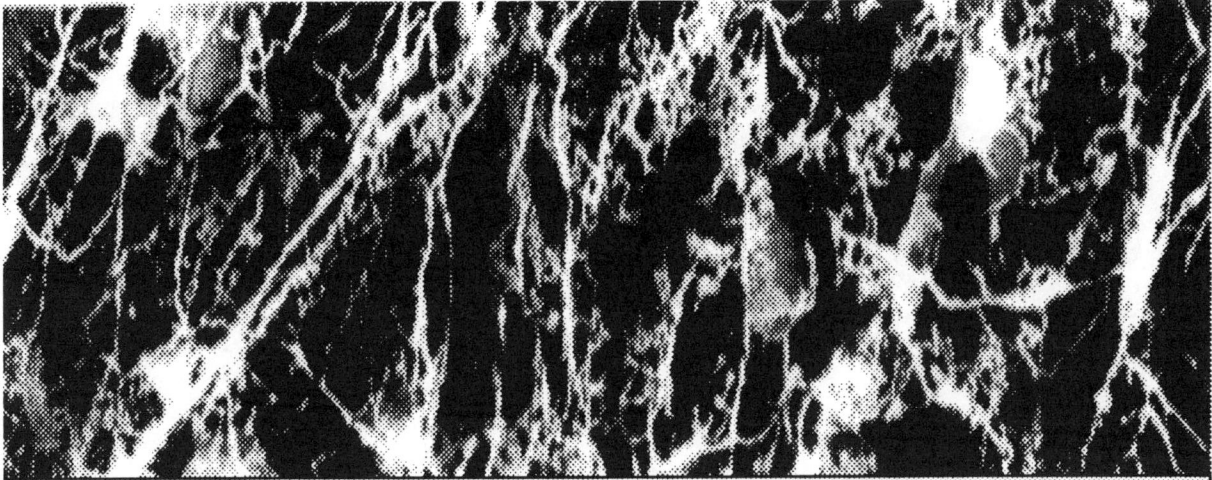

APPENDIX   A

FIELD EXPERIENCE
SYLLABUS

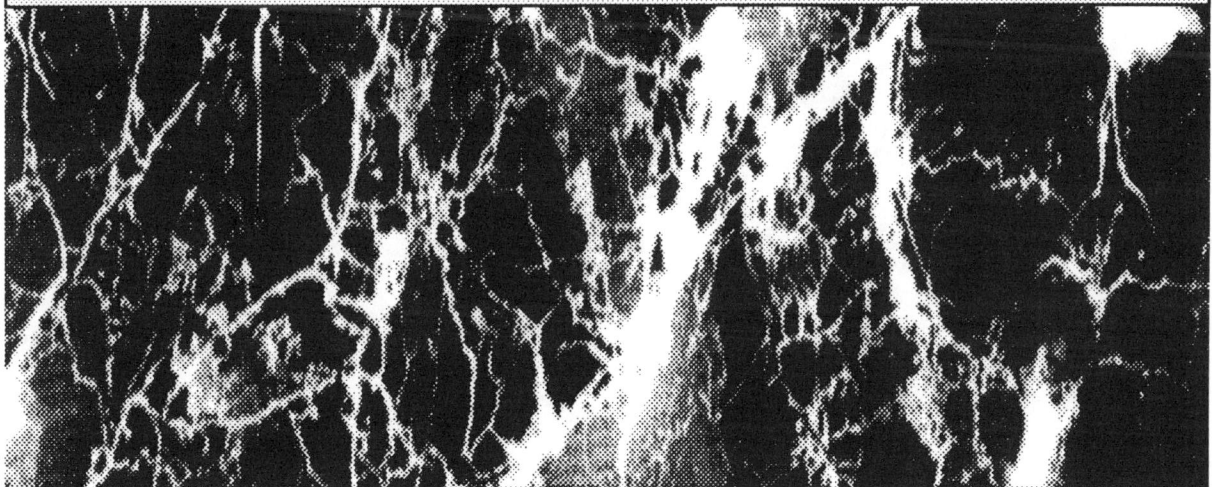

BOWLING GREEN STATE UNIVERSITY
SCHOOL OF HEALTH, PHYSICAL EDUCATION AND RECREATION
SPORT MANAGEMENT DIVISION

FIELD EXPERIENCE IN SPORT MANAGEMENT
SMD 489

SCHEDULE FOR RECEIPT OF WRITTEN WORK BY YOUR UNIVERSITY
SUPERVISOR WILL BE MAILED TO YOU AT THE BEGINNING OF YOUR
FIELD EXPERIENCE. PLEASE ENTER THE ASSIGNED DATES IN THE
APPROPRIATE BOXES BELOW.

WRITTEN WORK   DATE DUE IN UNIVERSITY SUPERVISOR'S
                               OFFICE

PROJECT OUTLINE ——————————

SUPERVISOR'S MIDSEMESTER ————
EVALUATION

OBSERVATION REPORTS (2)
PROJECT
PORTFOLIO
SUPERVISOR'S FINAL EVALUATION
EVALUATION OF SELF, AGENCY,
 AND SUPERVISOR
MATERIAL DESCRIBING AGENCY
 AND SUMMARY REPORT
SUMMARY OF EXIT INTERVIEW

* NOTE *   CONSIDER SENDING YOUR PROJECT, PORTFOLIO, ETC. VIA A
           COMMERCIAL COURIER SERVICE. THIS MAY REDUCE YOUR COST AND
           PROVIDE FOR MORE TIMELY RECEIPT BY YOUR UNIVERSITY SUPERVISOR.

_____

COURSE OBJECTIVES:

Through experiences afforded by this course the student will be able to:

1.   Apply theories and principles to specific situations.

2.   Demonstrate a growing awareness of organization and administrative structure, techniques, and procedures.

3.   Work successfully with a variety of personalities and groups.

4.   Demonstrate professional behavior.

5.   Exhibit effective communication skills.

6.   Display effective organizational and time management skills.

7.   Demonstrate creativity, initiative, and responsibility.

8.   Accept and utilize constructive suggestions to improve performance.

9.   Demonstrate self-confidence and leadership skills.

10. Evaluate oneself in regard to the transition from student to professional.

COURSE REQUIREMENTS:

The student will:

1.   Spend a minimum of <u>40 hours per week</u> in leadership and managerial tasks assigned by the agency supervisor for a period of <u>15 consecutive weeks</u>.

2.   Participate in additional job-related activities that will be a professional benefit.

3.   Submit work schedule(s) to the University Supervisor. A new schedule will be submitted each time the student's hours and/or location change. Students should use forms provided in the packet.

4.   Complete and submit a typed log each week to the faculty supervisor. Logs should be received by the faculty supervisor no later than Tuesday of each week. Students should retain a copy of their logs for their portfolios.

5.   Students [fall and spring semesters] working at agencies within a 50-mile radius of campus are expected to attend two (2) seminars. Specific dates,

time, and location of these seminars will be announced by the faculty supervisor. This requirement does not apply to summer session. However, individual faculty supervisors may schedule seminars at their discretion during summer sessions.

6. Arrange to be observed on the job at regular intervals by your agency supervisor(s).

7. Arrange with the faculty supervisor to be observed at the work site, provided student is located within a 3 1/2 hour driving radius of Bowling Green. With the first log, students should provide a detailed map, including directional orientation, from Bowling Green to their location.

8. Confer with the agency and faculty supervisor on a regular basis.

9. Complete two observations at other agencies. These observations should be made at agencies whose functions are closely associated with student's career goals. All arrangements will be made by the intern. A 2-4 page typed report will be completed for each agency visited. The report should include: agency name, complete address, telephone number, name and title of person interviewed, reason for selecting the agency, purpose of agency, questions asked, answers received, and overall perception of the agency.

10. Complete a significant indepth project. The idea for the project may be generated by the student or jointly with the agency supervisor; however, the work presented must be the student's own. Examples of possible projects include: facilities renovation/design, facility usage study, promotional concept and materials, case study, program development and evaluation, media guide, policies and procedures manual, cost analysis, market research, fund raising, fitness assessment and prescription, community relations activity, and grant writing. This project must be well conceived and of benefit to the student and the agency.

    PROJECT OUTLINE: The student mustsubmit a detailed typed outline of the proposed project to the university supervisor. The date for submission is specified on the schedule of receipt of written work (page 1). The outline must include purpose of project, how it will benefit student and the agency, exactly what will be included in the project, and in some situations, how the student will evaluate the impact of the project (i.e., fund raising or program development).

The university supervisor will approve or disapprove the project idea based on this outline. This decision and any suggestions for improvement will be conveyed to the student in writing.

PROJECT: Students should organize and present their projects as part of the portfolio. They should format the project presentation as follows: title, table of contents with page numbers, project as approved by the university supervisor, appendices containing supplemental materials (raw data, etc.). Sources of information used to complete the project must be properly documented.

11. Complete student, agency, and agency supervisor evaluations using the forms provided in the packet. Include these in the portfolio.

12. Develop a portfolio. Date for submission is indicated on page 1. Please organize your materials in a large loose-leaf notebook. Use dividers to designate and separate sections. This presentation will include your project, copies of your weekly logs, observation reports, copies of midsemester and final evaluations, additional materials you have prepared individually or jointly, student's evaluation of the field experience, evaluation of agency and agency supervisor, and results of exit interview. Please arrange to pick up your portfolio during exam week or by the end of the second week of the following semester or summer session. If this is impossible, please make arrangements with your supervisor to have your work mailed to you. Portfolios not picked up or mailed according to the above deadline will be destroyed.

13. Satisfactory completion of the agency experience. The will be demonstrated by the agency supervisor's midsemester and final evaluations. The student is responsible for conveying the evaluation forms to the agency supervisor and having them forwarded to your University supervisor by the specified dates.

14. Successfully complete other assignments pertinent to the experience.

15. Request an exit interview with your agency supervisor. Present a typed summary of this interview in your portfolio.

16. Compile descriptive material that is representative of the agency with which you are working. Printed materials might include brochure, media guides, fact sheets, newsletters, club/employee center profiles. Accompany the material you gather with a typed summary report using the form in your packet. Include

information you believe would be of value to future students working with this agency. The information you supply will be placed in the Mary A. Watt Professional Development Center for use by future students. Please send this information with your profile--in a separate detached folder.

GRADING

You will receive a letter grade for the field experience. The work you present is expected to be of the highest professional quality. Your grade will be based on the following elements: weekly logs; observation reports (2); project outline; project; portfolio; evaluation of yourself, agency supervisor, and agency; and agency supervisor's midsemester and final evaluations.

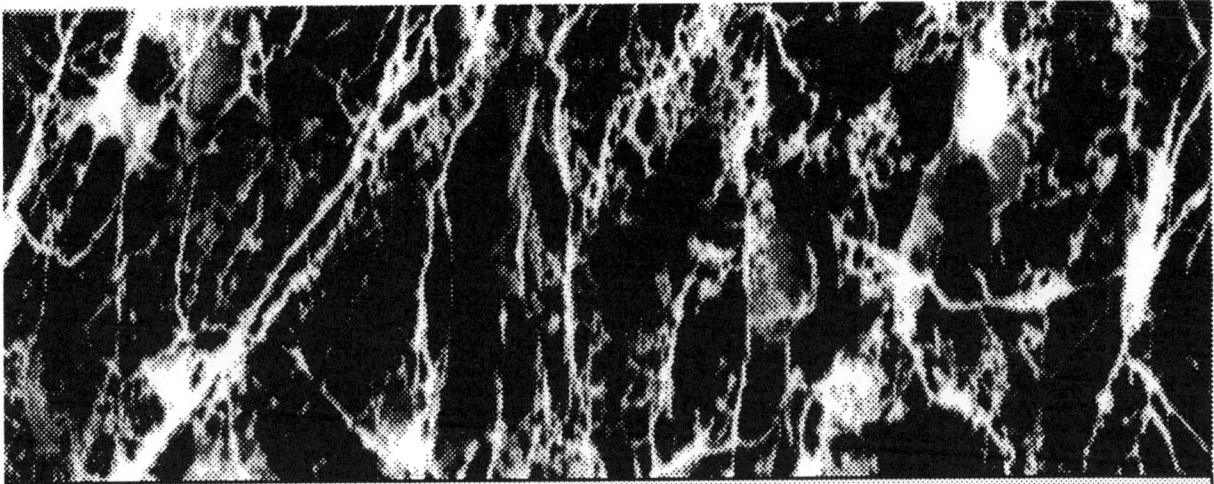

APPENDIX B

WORK SCHEDULE
AND WEEKLY LOG

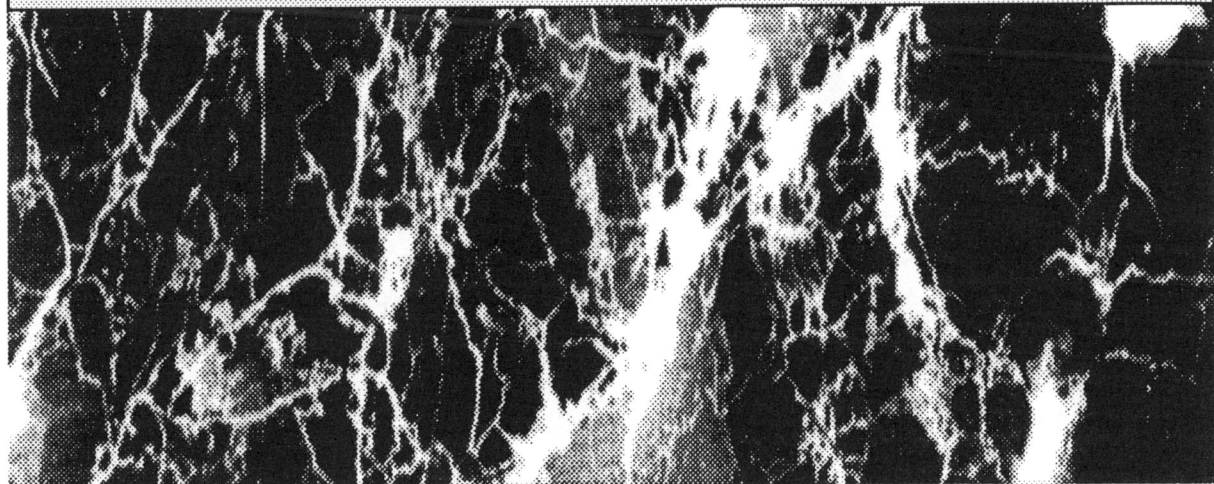

Semester _____ Name of Student _____

Week of _____ to _____ 19 ___ Location _____

BOWLING GREEN STATE UNIVERSITY
SCHOOL OF HPER
SPORT MANAGEMENT DIVISION
FIELD EXPERIENCE WORK SCHEDULE

	Monday	Tuesday	Wednesday	Thursday	Friday	Saturday	Sunday
8:00 AM							
9:00							
10:00							
11:00							
12:00 N							
1:00 PM							
2:00							
3:00							
4:00							
5:00							
6:00							
7:00							
8:00							
9:00							
10:00							
11:00							

Location, if different from above:

86

BOWLING GREEN STATE UNIVERSITY
SCHOOL OF HPER
SPORT MANAGEMENT DIVISION

FIELD EXPERIENCE WEEKLY LOG

Name _____

* <u>Please Type and Retain</u>
<u>a Copy</u>

Week of _____ to _____ 19 ____

Faculty Supervisor _____

I. Please indicate the times you worked:

Monday	Tuesday	Wednesday	Thursday	Friday	Saturday	Sunday

II. Field Experience Location: _____

III. <u>Evaluation of previous week's experiences</u>:

    A. <u>A concise description of what you did each day</u>.

    B. <u>New experiences:</u>

C. <u>Skills and knowledge used</u>:

D. <u>Skills and knowledge areas in which you felt deficient</u>:

E. <u>Comments concerning your feelings and experiences</u>:

F. <u>Plans for improving your performance</u>:

G. <u>Situations you observed during the week that were interesting and/or beneficial to your pre-professional development</u>:

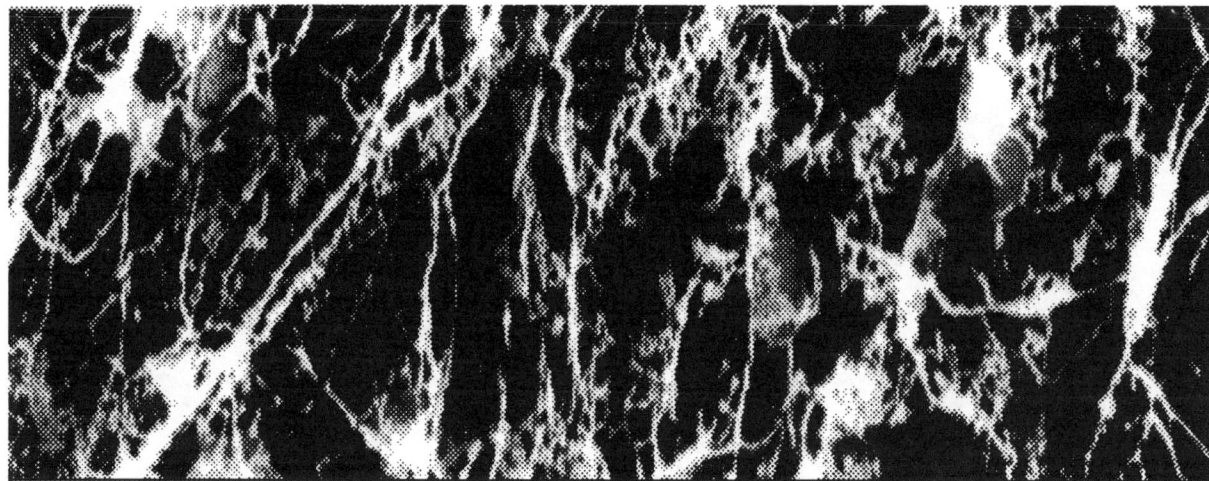

APPENDIX C

GUIDELINES FOR STUDENT EVALUATION OF THE FIELD EXPERIENCE

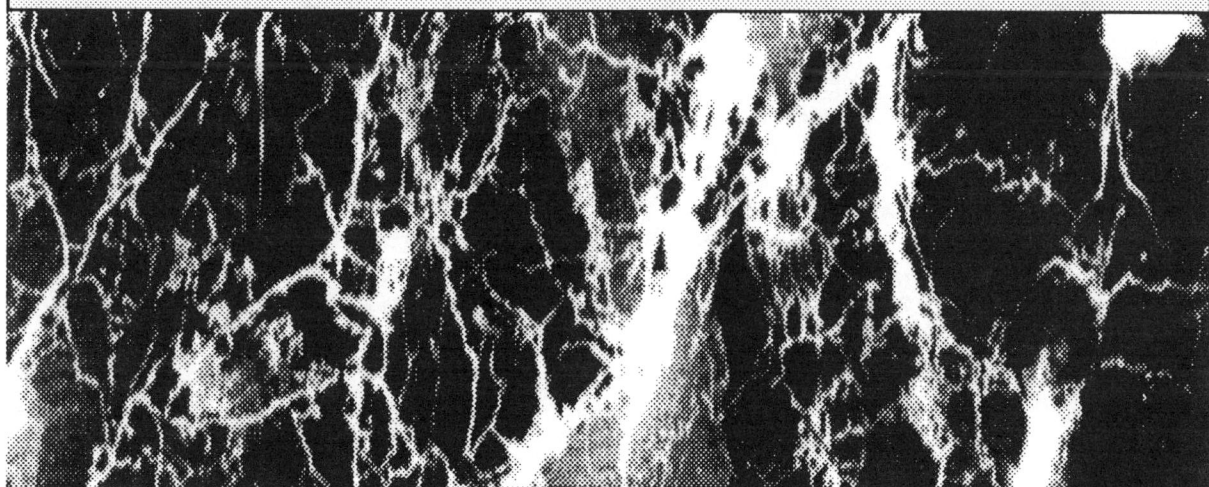

SPORT MANAGEMENT EVALUATION
* OUTLINE FOR STUDENT'S REPORT *

***** THIS REPORT MUST BE TYPED AND PRESENTED TO YOUR FACULTY SUPERVISOR ON THE DATE SPECIFIED ON THE SCHEDULE FOR RECEIPT OF WRITTEN WORK *****

I.   NAME, AGENCY, NAME OF AGENCY SUPERVISOR, AND DATE

II. SUMMARY: A brief description of your practicum experience.

III. IMPACT: What did you learn about yourself?

In what areas did you experience the most personal growth?

In what areas did you experience the most professional growth?

What insights have you gained into the field of sport management?

Based on your practicum experience, what skills would you like to develop in preparation for your internship?

How has the practicum influenced your career goals? Please explain.

IV. EVALUATION: Did the practicum experience meet your personal expectations?

How would you assess your performance at the agency?

Would you recommend this site to future practicum students?

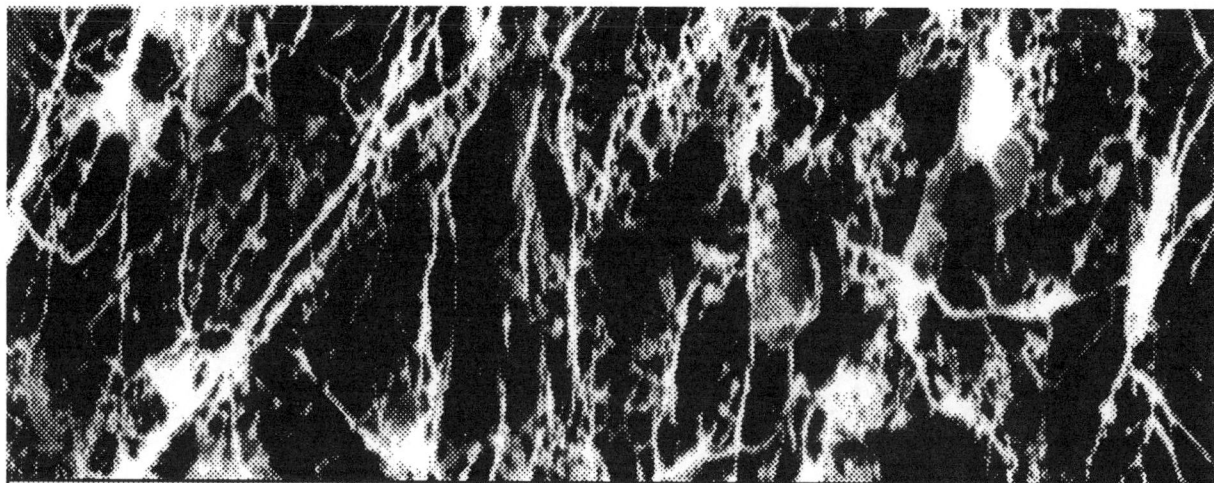

APPENDIX D

STUDENT EVALUATION OF THE SPONSORING ORGANIZATION

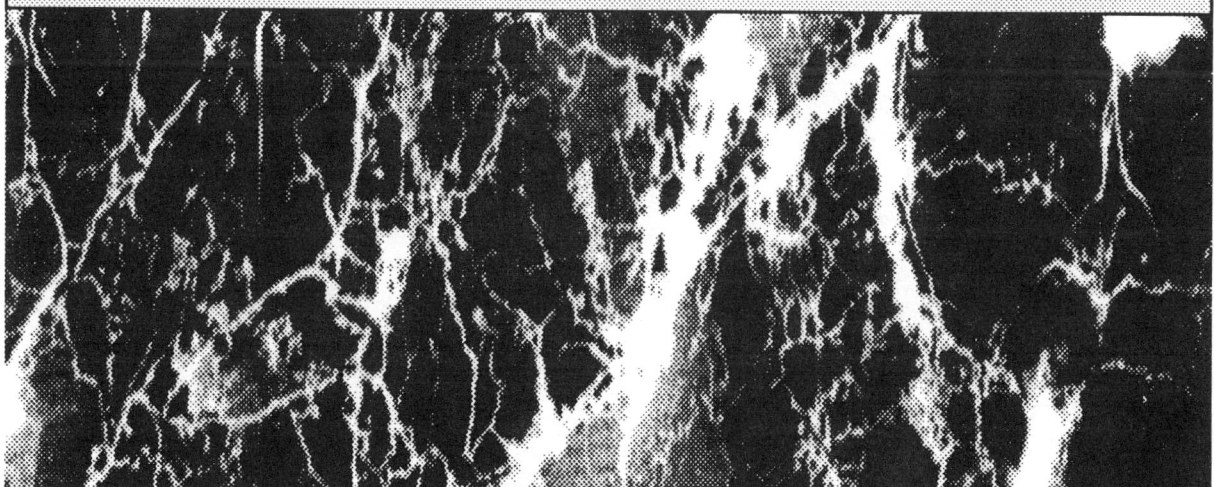

BOWLING GREEN STATE UNIVERSITY
SCHOOL OF HPER
SPORT MANAGEMENT DIVISION

EVALUATION OF THE AGENCY

Instructions: Please rate the strengths and weaknesses of the agency in terms of meeting your needs as an intern student. Use the following scale:

5 - excellent
4 - more than adequate
3 - adequate
2 - less than adequate
1 - poor
NA - not applicable

_____ 1. Acceptance of you as a functional member of the agency staff, willingness to integrate you into all appropriate levels of activities, programs, and projects.

_____ 2. Provision of relevant experiences in administration, supervision, and leadership.

_____ 3. Cooperation of agency staff to provide professional growth experiences through training programs, seminars, and other developmental activities.

_____ 4. Provision of assistance in helping you meet your personal and professional goals and objectives.

_____ 5. Possession of resources essential to the preparation of professionals (library, equipment, supplies, etc.).

_____ 6. Employment of qualified, professional staff with demonstrated capability to provide competent supervision.

_____ 7. Adequate scheduling of conferences with you and ongoing evaluation of your performance.

_____ 8. Allowance for relating classroom theory to practical situations.

_____ 9. Willingness to listen to suggestions or recommendations you might offer and willingness to discuss them with you, explaining the rationale for their acceptance or rejection.

Additional Comments - use other side if necessary:

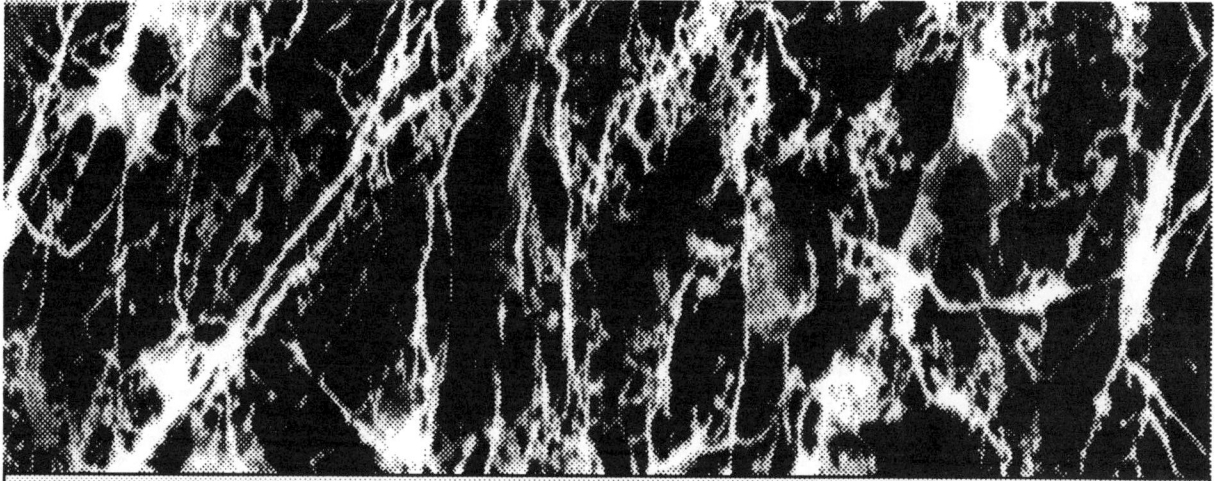

APPENDIX E

STUDENT EVALUATION
OF THE SITE SUPERVISOR

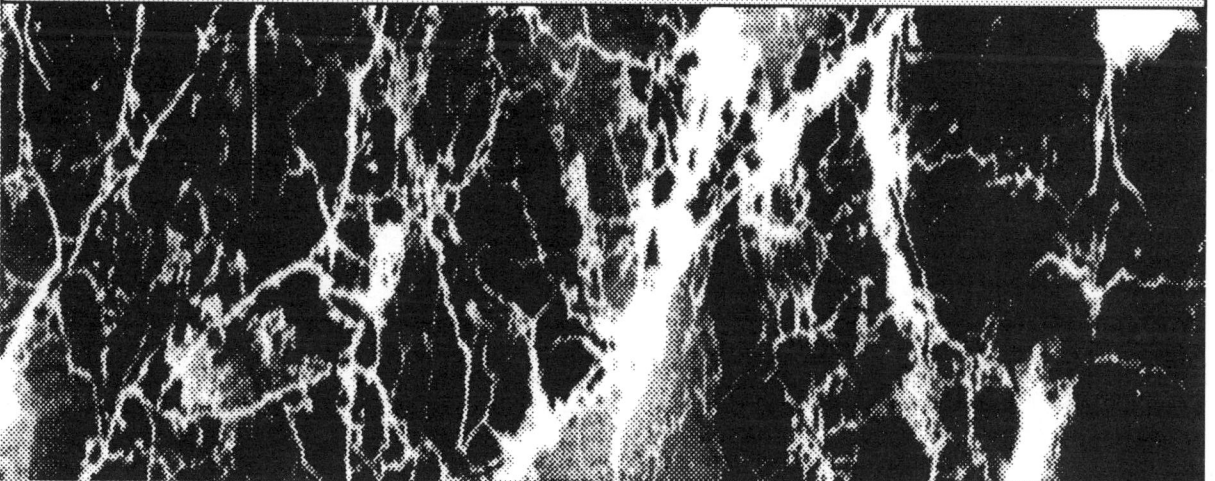

EVALUATION OF AGENCY SUPERVISOR

Instructions: Please rate the quality of supervision you received by your agency supervisor during the internship. Use the following scale:

5 - excellent
4 - more than adequate
3 - adequate
2 - less than adequate
1 - poor
NA - not applicable

_____ 1. Interest in you as a person and as a student intern.

_____ 2. Willingness to discuss the full range of activities at the agency.

_____ 3. Ability to respond to your problems and to help you work toward solutions.

_____ 4. Quality of conferences with agency supervisor.

_____ 5. Adequacy of arrangements made to orient you to the agency.

_____ 6. Sensitivity to your needs in accomplishing your objectives.

_____ 7. Expression of encouragement and sincerity.

_____ 8. Understanding of philosophy and practices in the profession.

_____ 9. Flexibility in arranging your task in light of changing situations within the agency and your increasing professional competencies.

_____10. Openness to change, innovation, and new techniques.

Additional Comments - use other side if necessary:

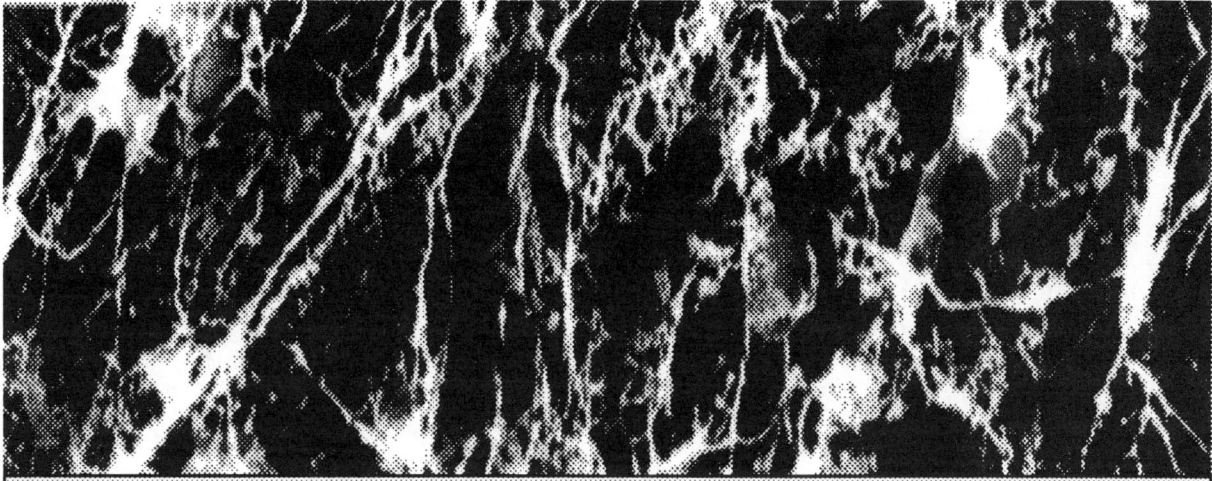

APPENDIX F

MIDTERM AND
FINAL EVALUATION
OF STUDENT (#1)

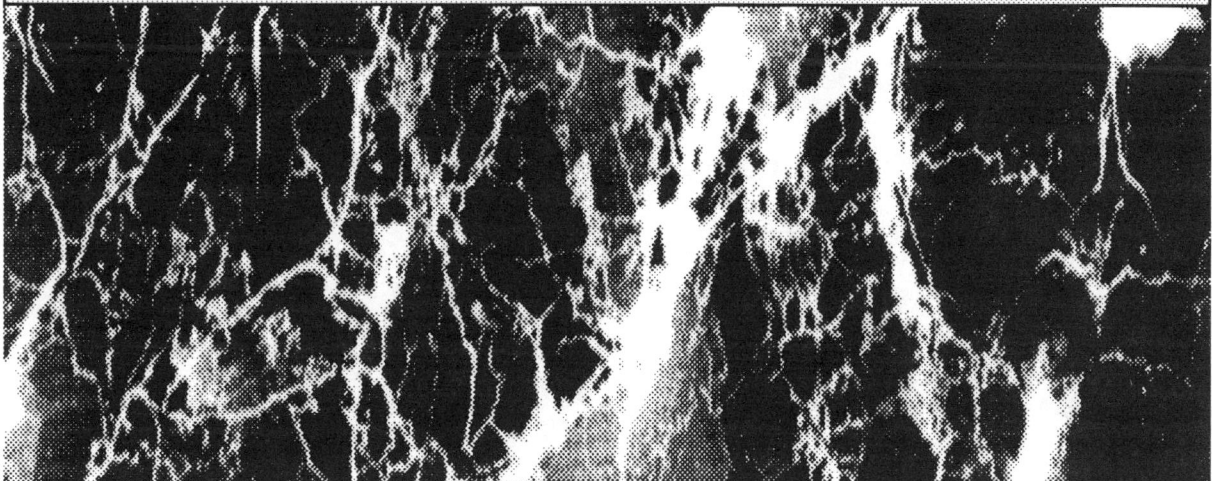

EVALUATION
DIVISION OF SPORT STUDIES AND MANAGEMENT
SCHOOL OF HEALTH, PHYSICAL EDUCATION AND RECREATION
BOWLING GREEN STATE UNIVERSITY

Please type or use black ink

Intern _____ Date _____

Organization/Agency _____

Address _____

                                                                                Zip

Supervisor _____ Phone (___) _____

                                                                        Area

Description of Intern's Responsibilities: _____

_____

_____

Please check: ☐ Midsemester Evaluation   ☐ Final Evaluation

          Date Due [_____]   Date Due [_____]

Please evaluate the intern by checking the appropriate rating and providing comments on each area of performance. If an evaluation area is not applicable in your situation, please check NA.

	Superior	Above Average	Average	Below Average	Poor	NA
Initiative and creativity						

Comments:

_____

	S	AA	A	BA	P	NA
Dependability and responsibility						

Comments:

_____

	S	AA	A	BA	P	NA
Leadership ability:						

Comments:

_____

104

	Superior	Above Average	Average	Below Average	Poor	NA
Time management skills						

Comments:

_____

	S	AA	A	BA	P	NA
Ability to organize and carry out task						

Comments:

_____

	S	AA	A	BA	P	NA
Ability to work with agency personnel						

Comments:

_____

	S	AA	A	BA	P	NA
Ability to understand and provide for client needs						

Comments:

_____

	S	AA	A	BA	P	NA
Ability to accept and utilize suggestions to improve performance						

Comments:

_____

	S	AA	A	BA	P	NA
Enthusiasm and self-confidence						

Comments:

_____

	Superior	Above Average	Average	Below Average	Poor 105	NA

Ability to communicate

Written:

Oral:

Comments:

_____

	S	AA	A	BA	P	NA

Professional appearance and behavior

Comments:

	S	AA	A	BA	P	NA

Overall I would evaluate the intern as:

Additional Comments:

Did you discuss this evaluation with the student? Yes _____   No _____

Date: _____   Signature: _____

Position: _____

****

Program Evaluation:

In what areas do you think the undergraduate intern might have been better prepared?

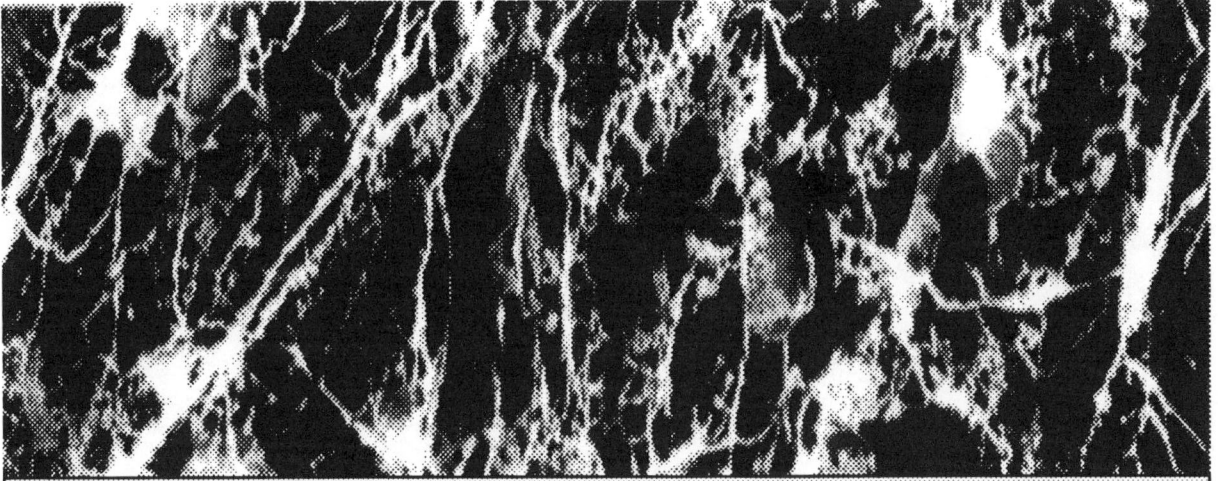

APPENDIX   G

MIDTERM AND
FINAL EVALUATION
OF STUDENT (#2)

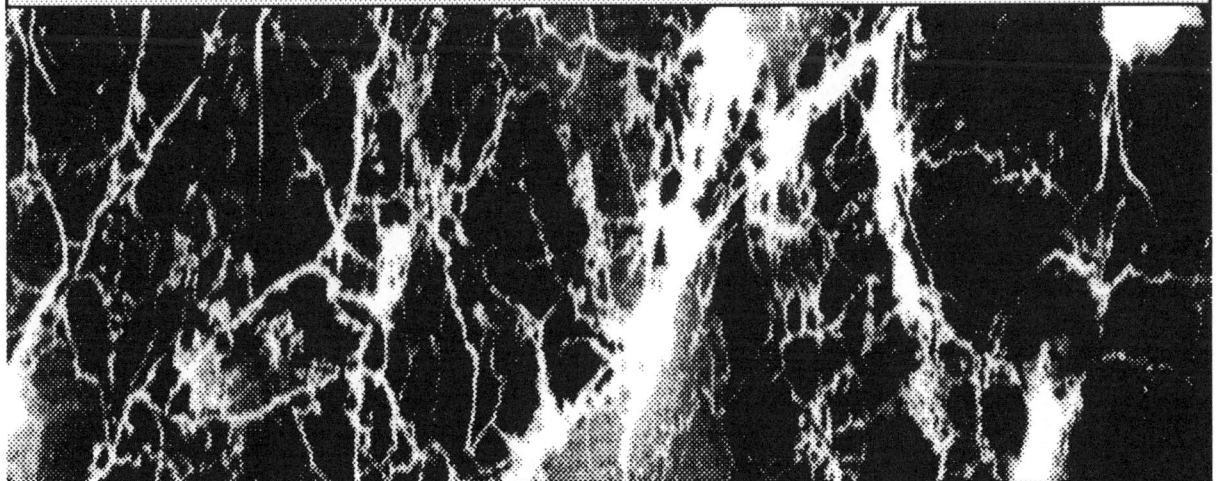

INTERN EVALUATION

Name _____

(_____) Date _____

Midsemester ☐   Final ☐

(_____) Date _____

PERFORMANCE AREA	NEEDS IMPROVEMENT			SATISFACTORY			VERY GOOD			EXCELLENT	
	1	2	3	4	5	6	7	8		9	10
ABILITY TO ORGANIZE AND CARRY OUT TASK SCORE [___]	Has some difficulty organizing and carrying out assigned tasks.			Manages to organize and carry out most assigned tasks in a competent manner.			Very well organized and carries out assigned tasks in a professional manner.			Exceptionally well organized. Carries out assigned tasks in an exemplary manner.	

Comments:

	1	2	3	4	5	6	7	8		9	10
QUALITY OF ASSIGNED WORK SCORE [___]	Below expectations. Needs frequent instruction and supervision. Work completed is less than satisfactory.			Meets expectations. Needs some supervision. Quality of work is competent.			Usually exceeds expectations. Needs very limited supervision. Work is of very good quality.			Consistently exceeds expectations. Work is always of highest quality.	

Comments:

	1	2	3	4	5	6	7	8		9	10
TIME MANAGEMENT SCORE [___]	Procrastinates much of the time. Does not complete most tasks in a timely manner.			Average ability to manage time on tasks. Some procrastination but most tasks are completed on time.			Very efficient in managing time on tasks. All tasks are completed on schedule.			Exceptional ability to manage time on tasks. Most work is completed ahead of schedule.	

Comments:

PERFORMANCE AREA	NEEDS IMPROVEMENT			SATISFACTORY			VERY GOOD			EXCELLENT	
	1	2	3	4	5	6	7	8		9	10
ABILITY TO COMMUNICATE ORALLY SCORE [ ]	Has difficulty conveying information/ideas to individuals and groups. Does not seem to be comfortable with oral communication.			Can competently express information/ideas to individuals and groups. Reasonably comfortable in most situations.			Very effective conveying information/ideas to individuals and groups. Comfortable during oral communication.			Exceptional ability to communicate information/ideas effectively to individuals and groups. Very comfortable and confident during oral communication.	

Comments:

	1	2	3	4	5	6	7	8		9	10
ABILITY TO COMMUNICATE IN WRITING SCORE [ ]	Below expectations. Has difficulty conveying information/ideas in writing. Numerous errors.			Can satisfactorily convey information/ideas in writing. Usually free of errors.			Very effective in conveying information/ideas in writing. Errors are rare.			Exceptional ability to communicate information/ideas in writing. Work is free of errors.	

Comments:

	1	2	3	4	5	6	7	8		9	10
DEPENDABILITY AND RESPONSIBILITY SCORE [ ]	Sometimes fails to complete work. Requires a lot of supervision in order to produce work.			Can be counted on to have task completed when required. Sometimes needs some supervision to do so.			Can always be counted on to have tasks completed. Is conscientious in performance of all assigned duties.			Exceptionally dependable and responsible in all circumstances.	

Comments:

	1	2	3	4	5	6	7	8		9	10
INITIATIVE AND ENTHUSIASM SCORE [ ]	Must be pushed to get projects started and completed. Does not display enthusiasm for assigned work.			Usually enthusiastic about work assignments. Sometimes waits for assignments and projects rather than taking initiative.			Self-starter. Makes the most of opportunities. Enthusiastic and requests additional responsibilities.			Consistently exceeds expectations in this area. Regularly requests opportunities to explore new assignments and projects. Makes the most of every opportunity.	

Comments:

PERFORMANCE AREA	NEEDS IMPROVEMENT			SATISFACTORY			VERY GOOD		EXCELLENT	
	1	2	3	4	5	6	7	8	9	10
ABILITY TO WORK WITH OTHERS IN THE ORGANIZATION SCORE [＿]			Usually gets along with people in the organization. Rarely initiates contact with other person and could be more outgoing.			Gets along well with people in the organization. Usually initiates contact with other personnel. Usually outgoing.		Very good relationship with personnel at all levels of contact. Interaction is positive and productive.		Exceptionally good relationships with personnel at all levels. Interaction is positive, productive, and sensitive to the needs of others.

Comments:

PERFORMANCE AREA	1	2	3	4	5	6	7	8	9	10
PROFESSIONAL APPEARANCE AND BEHAVIOR SCORE [＿]			Needs to be reminded frequently about appropriate attire and behavior in the work setting.			Seldom needs to be reminded of appropriate attire and behavior in the work setting.		Appearance and behavior is always appropriate to the work setting.		Appearance and behavior is exceptional and worthy of emulation by others.

Comments:

PERFORMANCE AREA	1	2	3	4	5	6	7	8	9	10
ABILITY TO ACCEPT AND UTILIZE SUGGESTIONS TO IMPROVE PERFORMANCE SCORE [＿]			Almost always rejects or discounts suggestions to improve performance. Rarely, if ever, attempts to utilize the suggestions.			Usually accepts suggestions to improve performance. Usually successful in utilizing suggestions.		Always welcomes suggestions to improve performance. Makes a concerted effort to utilize the suggestions.		Always welcomes and solicits suggestions to improve performance. Exceptionally successful in this endeavor.

Comments:

Additional Evaluative Comments:

_____   Signature of Evaluator _____

TOTAL SCORE [＿]

Note: The format of this evaluation instrument is based on <u>Associate Performance Review for Hourly Store Personnel</u> by Hook-SupeRx. Cincinnati, OH: Hook-SupeRx, Inc. Adapted by permission.

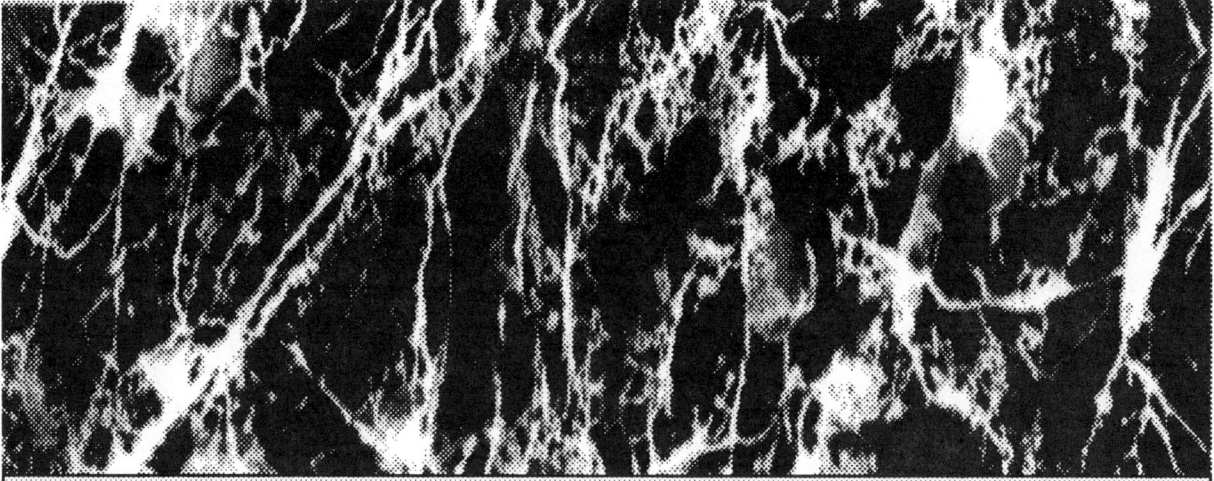

APPENDIX H

REPORTS FROM THE FIELD

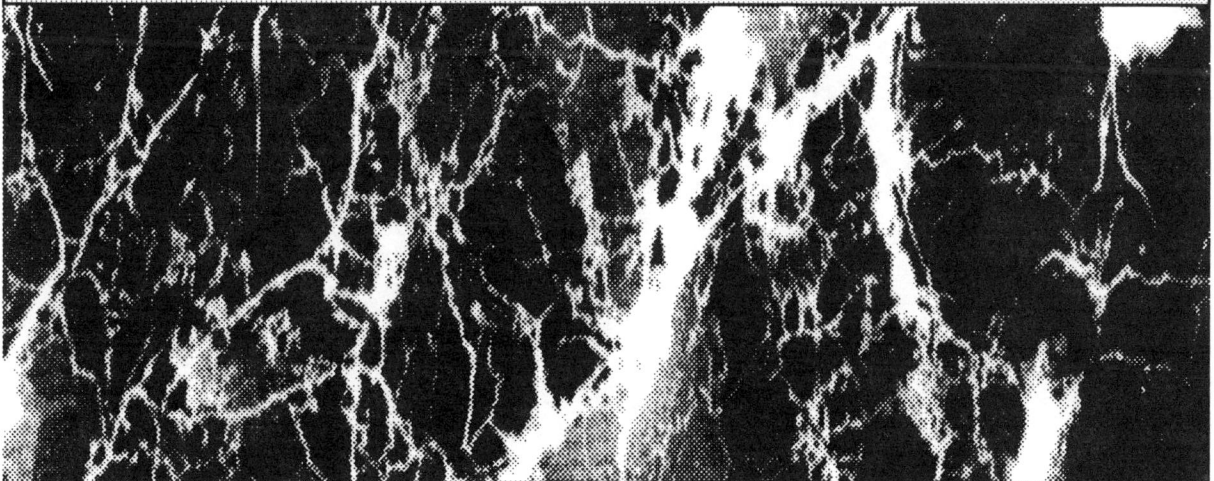

Report From the Field # 1

Sue A. Hager

Report From the Field: University Supervising
Sue A. Hager
Assistant Professor Emeritus of Health, Physical Education, and Recreation
Bowling Green State University

The field experience courses within the major sport management curriculum are vital to the overall professional preparation of students. It is during these experiences that each student has an opportunity to make application of the various theories and principles they have learned .

The practicum and internship experiences must be considered stringent academic course work. As with any university course there is an instructor assigned. By assigning a university faculty supervisor, it reinforces the academic value placed on this experience.

The faculty supervisor is the link for each student between the field experience site and the accrediting university. Student know there is an assigned faculty member to whom they are responsible. This faculty member is also available for assistance to the student. The university supervisor works closely with the agency supervisor to be sure the placement is a learning experience for the university student. The agency supervisor also has a contact person with the university. This setting assures the agency that the university has the best interest of both parties in mind when the contract is signed.

It is the responsibility of the university supervisor to work closely with each student. This contact is made by telephone a minimum of once every 10 days. During this phone contact the supervisor will talk with the student about the experiences this student is receiving; the phone conversation is also a follow-up of the weekly written log submitted by the student and very importantly gives the student an opportunity to express any positive experiences. If the student is experiencing any negative experiences, this is most assuredly discussed. If the university supervisor is a good listener then the supervisor will be able to detect concerns the student may have.

It is imperative that students not be made to feel they have been "hung out to dry." Students must begin to accept responsibility, but the university must not abandon them for the duration of the field experience.

While dealing with the student the university supervisor must also work very closely with the agency supervisor. After all, if the agency does not accept the student then this academic experience does not exist. The university supervisor must establish a good rapport with the agency supervisor. This is done either by phone conversation or when possible by actual visitation to the site. In either situation, the agency must be assured that the supervisor wants the experience to be two pronged. If the student learns and grows and the agency benefits from the knowledge and expertise brought by the student, then the result is twofold. By using common sense and intuition learned through teaching experience, the agency and university come to an understanding of the value, importance, and the success of such an apprenticeship.

Distance plays a major role in the contact between student and the university supervisor. The ideal setting is for each student to receive at least one on-site visit by the university supervisor. The one-on-one contact is beneficial to all parties. During the visit there should also be time allotted for private as well as three-way conversations involving agency supervisor, university supervisor, and university student.

In addition to the phone and site visits, the academic aspect must include written work. This work must be based on sound, solid functionality. The agency must know of the requirements of the university and be willing and able to support some type of in-depth written document.

It is important to understand the agency's need when establishing the written portion of the assignment. The university student provides an opportunity for the agency to add an extra pair of hands and a vibrant, progressive mind to its operation. With mutual agreement between the agency supervisor and the student and with the university supervisor's approval, a concept evolves and a final document is developed.

The evaluation is ongoing by the agency. It is put into written form as midterm and final evaluations. These forms should have been developed by the university and supplied by the student to the agency. Because this is an experience for the students, they too shall have an opportunity for evaluation. Each student is expected to grow and mature as a result of this experience; therefore, each must be given the opportunity for input.

The value of the university supervisor cannot be separated from the whole field experience. This person is a vital spoke in a three-spoke wheel. Without the student there is not a reason for the sport management major. Without the agency there is not an opportunity for "hands on" field experiences. Without the university faculty supervisor there is no vital academic component to justify the inclusion of field experiences into the curriculum. Thus the wheel is complete.

Report From the Field # 2
President of XXX Promotions

Report From the Field: Site Supervising
President of XXX Promotions

XXX Promotions is a small company that operates a series of nationwide summer outdoor basketball tournaments for youth and seniors. The business is less than 10 years old and is owned by two partners who play active roles in the management of the company. XXX Promotions employs two full-time employees in addition to the owners and two part-time employees (secretary and bookkeeper). Full-time employees and one part-time employee travel extensively during June, July, and August leaving only one part-time employee and the secretary to operate the home office.

We were approached by a senior sport management student who wanted to complete a summer internship with our company. During his interview, he was energetic, personable, seemed competent in interpersonal skills, indicated that he thought he was competent in telephone communication skills, had performed well in some marketing and promotion classes, and showed interest in and enthusiasm for our operation. We never considered using an intern but knew of other companies that did, and they were happy with the intern's work. We decided that we could offer the student a good experience and he could help us with home office management during our numerous absences. We did not realize the commitment we had made to our intern until some documents stating our duties arrived from his sport management professor, but we were willing to honor the requirements of performance reviews, evaluations, reports, and other activities requested. In fact, we decided that we should consult with our intern's college professor to write official internship job descriptions and specifications.

We decided that our intern should spend the first week getting acquainted with the office and the way we do things, so we did not structure his duties. We thought he should spend time reading our promotional materials and itinerary. Generally we wanted him to get comfortable with our environment.

On his first day, he was more quiet than at his interview and did not make much effort to interact with his colleagues. He was attempting to relocate temporarily to our area, and the information we gave him about the better areas of our city that might fit his budget was the only real contact we had with him. The second day was no different. He sat and reviewed the materials we had given him, asked no questions, made no effort to fit in, and took no initiative to help even though our staff was preparing to travel to a tournament site. The hectic pace of our office may have intimidated him, and perhaps we could have been more hospitable; we decided to make that a priority when we returned. On the intern's third day, one part-time employee and the secretary were the only permanent staff in the office.

Upon returning, we were told by the intern that he had been in contact with his professor and had gained approval to report to our worksite only periodically. The bulk of his assignment would be to prepare a promotions/public relations plan for our company. It seemed unusual to us, but having never worked with interns or colleges previously, we didn't protest because we thought that it was standard operating procedure although we didn't know how he could have a good internship by working by himself at home.

During the third week, I was contacted by the intern's college professor. She seemed especially pleased that we had allowed the intern to write our promotional plan. I responded that our company was always open to new ideas and if the intern could write a workable plan, we would use parts of it in our PR work. She asked if he was demonstrating some independence in his work; I responded that he certainly was and would have to since we travel so frequently. She suggested that he should travel with us occasionally in order to gain wider experiences. This was arranged, and the intern traveled to New York with us at the end of that week. He performed errands as requested.

I did not see the intern during the fourth week since he was working on his promotional plan at home. I was informed by the secretary that the college professor had called and wanted to arrange a visitation when I would be present. I indicated to the secretary that she should check my schedule and make the arrangements if I happened to be out when the professor called back. She said that she would handle it and indicated that she would have to remember to notify the intern when he called for his afternoon check-in. She then informed me that the intern had been making late-morning and afternoon calls to our office in order to see if his college professor had attempted to contact him. The intern had asked the secretary to tell the professor that he was out on an errand; she would then call him at his family home (located in a different part of the state), and he would eventually return the call to his professor.

The professor called me a few days later and told me the following story: The intern had complained to her that our company staff had ignored him for the first few days of his assignment, and in his frustration, he had contacted her for advice. Because his formal assignment at our company had been to assist in promotions, the professor suggested to him that he should write an outline for a strategic promotions plan and present it to us. That might enable him to learn about the company and interact with us. The intern told her that he had written an outline and that I did not approve of it. He told his professor that I had also told him that there was nothing he could do for us, and he could come and go as he wished; we would cover for him if his professor contacted him.

He eventually admitted to her that he had made up the work hours and duties that he had reporting on his weekly logs, except for the New York trip. He told her that he was confessing now because of her impending visitation to our company. I assured her that his story was not accurate, except for the fact that we did not have a lot for him to do during the first days, but it was due to our inexperience not our lack of interest.

The professor met with the student and discussed several options with him. He decided that he should delay his internship until the next semester rather than try to fit back into our company at this point.

I told her that we would still like to have interns from her program, but we would be more cautious and thoughtful in our selection. We know of other companies that take interns and have a selection process to choose them as they choose new employees. We have asked the college to help us in mapping out our procedure for intern selection. We look forward to working with them and their students. We are convinced that a good intern could be the solution to our home office understaffing problem, and we are likewise convinced that, with guidance from the college faculty, our company could provide some good, real-life experiences to an intern.

Report From the Field # 3
Jack W. Gregory

**Report From the Field: Coordinating the Selection and
Assignment Procedure for Field Experience Students
Jack Gregory, Athletic Director
Bowling Green State University,**

My first experience working with interns at Bowling Green State University was in 1982. I was very pleased and very excited about it. I believe in the hands-on approach because it is impossible for us to foresee the daily problems that come up in an Athletic Department. It is also impossible for us to plan for all the problems and troubles that might develop. The hands-on experience is possibly the best means of preparing for these problems. Not everyone in the Athletic Department was as excited as I was in regards to the internship program. However, I think their reservations centered around whether supervising an intern would take too much of their own individual time and whether they would be teaching the interns and, as a result, would not be accomplishing as much as they should. These doubts were soon dispelled.

It is possible for interns to work in a variety of positions within our administrative structure at Bowling Green. They might assist the Associate Director for Intercollegiate Affairs, who works with NCAA regulations, Mid-American Conference regulations, daily operations, the tutoring program, and other academic affairs. Other possibilities for internships are with the Assistant Director for Facilities and Event Management, the Assistant Director of Financial Affairs, the Athletic Development Director (Fund Raiser), the Athletic Promotions Director, the Sports Information Director, the Golf Course Director, or the Ice Arena Director. There are many different areas in which we can give an intern experience.

The selection and assignment procedure we use is quite well-defined. Some students will contact us directly asking about internships. We, in turn, send them back to the Sport Management Division of the School of Health, Physical Education and Recreation to obtain formal permission to apply to the Athletic Department. We then have a basic interview for them. The purpose of this interview is to ascertain their needs, their desires, their goals. After that, we try to match their interests with our needs and we make an assignment accordingly. We then bring them back for a second interview. This interview is with the Director of one of the various programs mentioned above. At that time, it is the Director's responsibility to inform the interns of their roles and assignments. From then, it is a regular work week. We do give them compensatory time because many of them will be working Saturdays. The person in the Financial Affairs Office, for instance, is working at the game ticket sales and that always involves evenings and/or Saturdays. So, we give them time off to compensate for the time that they have to put in beyond regular working hours.

We maintain updated reports on the interns, and it is the responsibility of the site supervisor (the person in the Athletic Department to whom the student is assigned) to handle the reports and evaluations for the Sport Management Division. In addition to the regular assignment, we give interns special assignments, such as last year's MAC Championship, working with the special tournaments, or possibly the Falcon Fun Run or some other event. We also, at times, will move them around in the Department from one particular assignment to another, especially if that is their choice.

Everyone in our Department knows my personal feelings on internships. It is very important for the interns to get worthwhile experience and we want them actually to be "thrown into it." We want them to be involved. We want them to participate in the activities in the same way the Director does. I can recall my experiences in my student teaching days. It was quite a few years ago, but my own experience is that student teaching had as much effect on molding me as a future teacher as anything else I had done in my undergraduate days. I think the same thing is true with internships in Sport Management. It would be very difficult for us to give students any kind of academic preparation to handle such situations as when we had the Toledo football game here and we had an overflow crowd. It was a great experience for the interns who were working to be involved in solving that problem and in the improvising and the adjusting that we had to do. The same thing holds true in many other events. Our MAC Spring Championships come to Bowling Green only once every ten years. As a result, an intern had the opportunity to work with that and had quite an experience or at least quite an experience as far as our Conference is concerned. So I do emphasize that I am a strong believer in the program and I am also very pleased with the type of individuals that we receive here at Bowling Green State University. I am not the promotions director for the Division, but I do think our Sport Management Division does a fantastic job! (Gregory, 1984)

Note. From "Coordinating the Selection and Assignment Procedure for Field Experience Students" by J. Gregory, in *Sport Management Curricula: The Business and Education Nexus* (pp. 84-85) by B. K. Zanger & J. B. Parks (Eds.), 1984, Bowling Green, OH: Bowling Green State University. Copyright © 1984 by Bowling Green State University. Reprinted by permission.

Report From the Field # 4

Robert Miller

Report From the Field: Sport Management Field Experiences with the Detroit Tigers Baseball Club
Robert Miller
Assistant Director of Public Relations, Detroit Tigers Baseball Club

In 1983, I created a successful internship program for the Detroit Tigers Baseball Club. Previously we had hired "gofers." This was our first venture into a formal program and our objective was to teach a student the business of public relations.

When formulating our program, I drew from my own internship experience. I had been a "gofer" in 1977 and this led to an unofficial internship in 1978 and a full-time position in 1979. The first phase of this project was to evaluate the needs of our public relations department. We also had a space problem because there were already five people in our office. I was responsible for defining the job and determining hours and the salary for this internship.

It was decided that our intent for this intern position would be to observe the Public Relations operation. It was apparent that the Tigers were learning how to run an internship program and that our first student intern would be our experimental subject. Our questions were: "What do we expect to get out of this program and what will be expected of us?" Any potential intern would be asking the same questions.

The answers from the Tigers' point of view were to teach public relations to a student, to give our intern exposure to a variety of facets of this occupation, and to promote the intern's confidence and self-assuredness which are two qualities employers desire. In return, we would ask our intern to observe, to absorb and to contribute. After all, we had as much to learn from our intern as he or she would learn from us. A program eventually evolved. Our intern would be asked to do small tasks until he or she was familiar with the way we operated. It was my intention to give our intern more freedom day by day until he or she might ultimately be able to work without supervision.

With this in mind, we set out to hire our intern. We were fortunate to be approached by Bob Zink, a student in Bowling Green's Sport Management Program, when we stopped in Toledo this past January during our annual Winter Press Tour. Bob met the criteria to qualify for field experience with us and we hired in March.

Because of our initial effort, I have more than enough applications to last into the 1990's. Therefore, I have set three criteria for selection of our future interns. First, a student in need of field experience will be given high priority. Second, it would be beneficial if our intern lived close to Detroit. Third, our intern will have to pass an intangible requirement: Will this person be able to handle pressure? Invariably there will be pressure, real and imagined.

We were fortunate that Bob Zink met all these criteria. As a first-time intern he may have had as much to do with the continuation of our program as anyone or anything. Bob was very willing to learn. He would come in at 1:00 for a 7:30 game and answer phones. This introduced Bob to dealing with the public. He was exposed to irate callers, gamblers, people who asked trivia questions, people who asked the impossible, and even a few people who had legitimate reasons to call. Bob learned how to run a copier, typewriter, calculator, and the telecopier, which are vital to sports public relations. Bob soon learned a valuable lesson: If you don't know the answer, at least know how or where to get the answer. The consummate employee will try to learn as much as possible. Over the course of the summer, Bob became acclimated to his surroundings. I was on hand in case he had any questions, but as I had hoped, Bob was able to learn on his own.

My program was taking shape. Bob was learning a great deal about media, interoffice and business relations. He had met a number of people in the course of his internship and was anxious to talk with anyone who was willing to talk with him. He was gaining invaluable experience on his own accord that I knew to be far more meaningful than anything I could say through a lecture. There were areas where I felt Bob could improve and I was learning from my mistakes. One thing we did have was a successful relationship, not of mentor and student, but of friend to friend. Because I was 26 and Bob was 23, we could relate well. We worked hard separately and together, all the time keeping the lines of communication open. I asked him at least once a week if his internship was what he expected and if he had any comments and criticisms.

The value of an undergraduate intern cannot be realized unless he or she is encouraged to contribute to the organization. I gave Bob a generally free hand after he had earned my trust. He then became assimilated into our department and was accepted by the other staff. The difference in Bob from April to October was tremendous. I asked for and received his input on a number of subjects. I believe the end result of our efforts was to have made Bob what I call an experienced veteran, ready to work for a professional sport organization. With the training he had been given, all he needed was a job.

In asking myself whether our program was a success for both Bob and the Tigers, I would have to say yes. Our intention was to teach a student the business of public relations. I think we fell short of completing that goal. But we were able to show Bob our method of operation and give him a taste of what it's like on the inside.

We have a few rough spots we have to smooth over, but with practice the Tigers hope to develop a first-rate internship, one that would be of equal value to the undergraduate sport management intern as well as the professional sport organization.

I do not think I completely answered my earlier questions. "What can we expect to get out of an internship program and what will be expected of us?" I believe we are too new at this to make a definitive statement. As long as there are students willing to learn, I believe the professional sport organization has an obligation to teach. Someday, the value of an intern will be measured. That rating will be a direct reflection upon us. (Miller, 1984)

Report From the Field # 5

William P. Bauza

Report From the Field: Values Of Field Experiences
William P. Bauza
Riverview Racquet Club, Eastlake, OH

Through personal experience I have come to believe that field work is, without a doubt, the most important part of every student's curriculum.

My fieldwork consisted of a three-credit-hour practicum at the Student Recreation Center at Bowling Green State University, a five-credit-hour practicum at a sporting goods store, and a twelve-credit hour internship at a racquet club.

While at the Student Recreation Center I worked with a women's fitness program. This practicum gave me the opportunity to design a recreation program for a specific clientele in a specific area of fitness.

At the sporting goods store, I began as a sales clerk and within two months was promoted to Assistant Manager. I held this position until graduation. Experience at this store allowed me to learn to cater to the retail needs of athletes and to learn about retail management. Inventory control, special orders, scheduling, and sales were all part of my job.

The internship at the racquet club was the highpoint of my undergraduate career. As Assistant Manager, I was involved with bookkeeping, budgeting, tournaments, leagues, program direction, scheduling, sales, public and member relations, food and beverage operations, and management of the club and staff.

My supervisors and their agencies composed an excellent pool of resources from which I was able to draw. Because of the diversity of my fieldwork I was able to learn, by comparison and contrast, more about the area of sport management than any structured course would allow.

Experience and maturity are the two areas that my fieldwork most enhanced by placing me in situations which required more responsibility and professionalism than coursework. It especially helped develop my written and verbal skills.

Students should not be apprehensive about field experience. It may not be easy to find these opportunities but with the help of faculty, alumni, and peers, fieldwork can be a very positive experience. (Bauza, 1984)

Note: From "Values of Field Experiences" by W. P. Bauza, in *Sport Management Curricula: The Business and Education Nexus* (pp. 93-94) by B. K. Zanger and J. B. Parks (Eds.), Bowling Green, OH: Bowling Green State University. Copyright 1984 by Bowling Green State University. Reprinted by permission.

Report From the Field # 6

Todd J. Pallo

**Report From the Field: Personal Statement on the Internship Experience
Todd J. Pallo
Field Experience Intern
Bowling Green State University**

I fulfilled the internship requirement at Advantage International in Washington, D C. I was required to find this internship on my own, which was beneficial for two reasons: (a) I learned first-hand the steps involved in obtaining an internship/job, and (b) I had the freedom to select my own sport-related agency. I pursued the position with Advantage International because I wanted to be associated with a highly reputable firm. There are three major divisions within Advantage International: (a) Athlete representation, (b) Event Marketing, and (c) Corporate Marketing. Because of the varied businesses of Advantage International, I thought I could benefit from the wide array of sport-marketing experiences.

I was fortunate in that I was never "treated like an intern" at Advantage (e.g., stuffing envelopes or making copies). Rather, I was part of the individual marketing team. I was given many experiences and opportunities. Some examples of my experiences were:

1. Much of my work experience concerned corporate research. A great deal of time was spent examining corporate literature and doing telephone work. It was very rewarding in that I acquired a tremendous understanding of the corporate decision-making process and the strategy therein. I was also exposed to the many facets of the service marketing-negotiation process.
2. Much of my research was concerned with attempts to get Team Rollerblade on a nationwide tour. I performed extensive market research on targeting the college population. I was also involved in the research and procurement of exhibition/ demonstration sites for a corporate-sponsored beach tour.
3. For a 2 to 3 week period, my efforts were devoted specifically to the demographic and market research associated with media buying. I experienced first-hand the steps involved in purchasing and placing media buys.
4. I performed an extensive cost analysis on forming a fan club (for a client). I also researched the strengths and weaknesses of several existing fan clubs and examined the process by which the clubs were developed.

As a result of this experience, I gained a thorough understanding and appreciation for the role played by market research. Additionally, I have personally added to my knowledge the "behind the scenes" efforts of sports marketing. I was constantly interacting with people both in person and on the phone. I observed a great improvement in my communication skills.

I have also affirmed that the sports industry is where I want to be. I knew this when I actually looked forward to coming into work every day ... without getting paid. Finally, I realized the importance of establishing contacts in the industry.

I cannot think of a more valuable tool for learning. The internship requirement is one of the strengths of my sport management curriculum. Internships are opportunities. Students should make the most of them.